SILENT WITNESSES IN THE GOSPELS

SILENT WITNESSES IN THE GOSPELS

Bible Bystanders and Their Stories

ALLAN F. WRIGHT

SERVANT
BOOKS

PUBLISHED BY ST. ANTHONY MESSENGER PRESS
CINCINNATI, OHIO

Scripture texts used in this work are taken from the New American Bible. The Old
Testament of the New American Bible copyright 1970 by the Confraternity of Christian
Doctrine (CCD), Washington, D.C. (Books 1 Samuel to 2 Maccabees, copyright 1969);
Revised New Testament of the New American Bible, copyright 1986 CCD; Revised Psalms
of the New American Bible, copyright 1991 CCD. All rights reserved.

Published by St. Anthony Messenger Press
28 W. Liberty St.
Cincinnati, OH 45202
www.servantbooks.com

Cover design by Brian Fowler/DesignTeam, Grand Rapids, Michigan

04 05 10 9 8 7 6 5 4 3 2

Printed in the United States of America
ISBN 1-56955-323-8

Library of Congress Cataloging-in-Publication Data

Wright, Allan F., 1964-
  Silent witnesses in the Gospels : Bible bystanders and their stories /
Allan F. Wright.
    p. cm.
  ISBN 1-56955-323-8 (alk. paper)
  1. Bible. N.T.--Biography. I. Title.
  BS2430 .W67 2002
  226'.0922--dc21

                                                                              2002009762

Dedication

For Desiree and her sustaining love.

To my parents, Ivan and Jane Wright:
With and without words you have shown me what love is.
To David and Diane, Nina and Todd,
Christopher, Cheri, and Charlie:
My laughter would be silenced without you.

With special thanks to Paul Thigpen,
who lovingly edited this work.

Contents

Foreword

I've known Allan for over seven years and, countless times, have heard him teach on the Scriptures. Even though I've been ordained for many years as a priest, *each time* I learn something new. His teaching is creative, alive, challenging, inviting, and insightful. Just like Jesus, Allan truly shares the Good News! I am thrilled to know that, through this book, thousands of others will be able to experience this gift. What I can assure you, also, is that the testimony of Allan's life is totally consistent with the Word he shares with you here. He is, truly, the "real thing" when it comes to being an apostle, an evangelist, and a missionary of the Lord Jesus in the power of the Spirit.

What, specifically, can you hope for from this book? Allan invites you to look deeper into the Word, to discover the hidden meaning there—what the early Church Fathers called the "mystery." Through his retelling of the story we get to experience it all from the perspective of the "little" people in the gospel, the ones that we don't hear from but who were the principal witnesses of these world-changing events. People like you and me! What were they thinking? What were they feeling? What sort of impact did this strange Jesus and His unorthodox teaching have on them?

As we listen to their stories, as Allan shares them with us, we start to see and hear the Word with clearer eyes and sharper hearing. We learn to pay attention to what's "between the lines," the unspoken word, the "aha" moments that must have moved and thrilled and changed hearts. From the shock of the waiters at the wedding feast in Cana to the weeping sinner woman pouring the precious oil over Jesus' feet, Allan demonstrates a unique talent for making the hidden story behind the story come alive.

In keeping with the best spiritual tradition in the Church, this isn't just another book to study but rather a book that invites you to pray with it. Allan combines the knowledge gained through an advanced scriptural degree, ongoing study, and extensive travel in the Holy Land with the communication skills of a gifted teacher and evangelist. Yet what is key in understanding these reflections is that they ultimately spring from Allan's own vital prayer life. They reflect insight that comes not just from the head but from the heart as well, a living encounter with the God who is ever new, fresh, young; always alive and vibrant.

So, the real invitation of this little volume is to *pray,* to find yourself once again refreshed and renewed with that Good, Good News—to feel yourself more alive—to savor your world, yourself, and others with a lighter, freer, more loving heart. May this be the blessing of this volume for you. It's the blessing that Allan has brought to all of us who know him! Peace!

Rev. Dennis M. Berry, S.T., Ph.D.
Co-Director, Fr. Judge Apostolic Center
Stirling, New Jersey
December 8, 2001, Feast of the Immaculate Conception

Acknowledgments

With appreciation and great joy to all of the administration, the faculty, and especially the students, both present and past, at Union Catholic High School, who have been an inspiration and a constant example of faith, hope, and love throughout the years.

In gratitude to the Missionary Cenacle Family and the friends at the Father Judge Center in Stirling, New Jersey, where faith and virtue are lived out each day under the guidance and power of the Holy Trinity. For the fellowship around both tables, Eucharistic and dinner, that have been a source of joy and nourishment.

Heartfelt thanks to my good friend Fr. Dennis Berry, S.T., who has modeled Jesus in his compassion and love for the poor and marginalized, who so often go unnoticed but never escape his notice.

Thanks as well to my friend Fr. John Morley, who has been a source of academic encouragement and scholarship since our first meeting at Seton Hall University.

To the diners throughout New Jersey, where many of these characters joined me for ham-and-cheese omelets.

"Be Good, Do Good, Be a Power for Good."
Fr. Thomas A. Judge

Christo
Vero
Regi

Introduction

No one is insignificant in the eyes of God. From the most saintly among us to the person whom you believe is the farthest away from God, no one escapes His notice, care, and love. Reading and studying the Scriptures has brought me into a deeper understanding of this love that God has for me and for the world, and for that I am most grateful.

In becoming familiar with the stories found in the Gospels and growing up in the Catholic Church, where the Word of God is held in the greatest of esteem, there can be a danger in not entering into the stories that are handed down to us, because they have become so recognizable, so familiar.

It is my hope that these reflections on the silent actions of men and women found in the Gospels will help with the process of entering into the story. My conjecture is simply that—conjecture. Speculations about what it was like to be there during the ministry of Jesus, through the eyes of men and women who too often go unnoticed. What were these people thinking right before and right after Jesus entered their towns, their lives?

In business negotiations it is often said that the devil is in the details. In Scripture I believe that God is in the details. While the Gospels were written so that we might come to faith in Jesus Christ, the men and women that are mentioned "around the action," as it were, are important and have a story to tell.

I bring my upbringing and viewpoints with me, as well as my study experiences, as I write about these characters. These reflections are not designed to make up a historically precise, "the way it was" piece but rather a point of departure for your own reflection.

These characters have become my friends over the years, the four friends of the paralytic, the servers at Cana, Jairus—I can picture them as clear as day as they come to terms with Jesus, themselves, and what it means to be a disciple. It is my hope that they will lead you closer to Christ and to your neighbor on your journey of faith, as they have led me.

I have added some possible applications to these silent actions and witnesses from my own experience but this is in no way an exhaustive list. I leave it to you and your community of faith to reflect on what these silent actions may be saying to you. As Pope Paul VI wrote in 1975, people today "are more impressed by witnesses than by teachers, and if they listen to these it is because they also bear witness" (*Evangelization in the Modern World,* 41).

ONE

Absolute Faith: Silent Servers at Cana

John 2:5-8

His mother said to the servers, "Do whatever he tells you." Now there were six stone water jars there for Jewish ceremonial washings, each holding twenty to thirty gallons. Jesus told them, "Fill the jars with water." So they filled them to the brim. Then he told them, "Draw some out now and take it to the headwaiter." So they took it.

Life is difficult. Hard labor, a short life expectancy, as well as primitive living conditions make life arduous, not to mention the fact that existence under Roman occupation is grueling. Yet the next few days will be different, because there will be a wedding. This will be a time of celebration, joy, and merriment with family and friends. The invitations have been made and the time of celebration is at hand.

The sound of music and festivities leads you right into the center of the celebration as you draw near in your finest clothes. As you approach, with the sun high in the sky, friends greet you with a smile and embrace, "Come along, we've been waiting for you." The bright, colorful garments are a pleasant change from the usual drab clothes you wear, and the vibrant colors add to the excitement that's in the air.

The father of the bride greets you with a kiss of peace and a strong embrace; his arms engulf you as his joy in meeting you is fully expressed: "You're looking well, my friend." Then he grabs you by the shoulder and says, "Join in the dancing and singing; today we celebrate!"

You have to tilt your head as you strain to hear him over the lively music being played by the musicians. The choicest foods and finest wine also greet all those invited to the celebration. The distinctive aromas of weddings and festivals past permeate the air and tempt the pallet. As you recline at the table with friends surrounding you on either side and music whirling through the air, you know that life is, indeed, good.

The taste of the wine rejuvenates your parched lips and taste buds while you observe the joy of the two families now together as one, and another container of wine is passed your way. The desert heat is forgotten and the day's labor is a distant memory as you delight in and enjoy this happy occasion.

You notice Jesus and His disciples wholeheartedly joining in the dancing. They can hardly contain their joy as they dance around, arm in arm, in a big circle. Their beards and clothes are slightly stained by the lavish foods and wine, but this does not inhibit their enthusiasm. "We should be invited to weddings every week," Peter is overheard saying to Jesus as he catches his breath. "I'll see what I can do about that," says Jesus, smiling. They both laugh and find their way to the table.

"Sir, come quickly," remarks the wine steward to the father of the bride in a somewhat loud whisper, "they have run out of wine!" The panicked look on their faces tells of the potential catastrophe. "Follow me," the father beckons as they both hurry down the path to the storage room. "I've been waiting for this day for many years," he says, staring at the empty jars of wine. "And now this, no wine—what will people say? My daughter, my family ... our reputation, the shame!"

The celebration is still going on but you begin to sense a tension in the air. You can't put your finger on it but you can see it on the face of the bride's father as he receives the news from a steward concerning the lack of wine. "Jesus," says Mary, "they have no more wine" (see Jn 2:3).

Jesus pauses; His gaze falls upon one of the servers. "What's your name?" He asks. "Eliab," replies the server. "Eliab, quickly, grab two of your friends and meet me in the storage room." Eliab calls two of his friends and they make their way around the back of the house, near the animal stalls, to the storage room.

"Fill these six stone jars with water at once." Jesus' voice is firm and direct, so the servers get right to the task, dragging the heavy vessels to the well about a stone's throw away without asking any questions. The sun is no longer high in the sky as the day turns toward evening. Without a word they do as He says, following the direction of Mary.

Their muscles are already sore as they make the trip to the well to fill the stone jars with one hundred and eighty gallons of water. They pull up the bucket from the well time and again.

"Eliab," his friend retorts, "are you sure this is what Jesus wanted?"

"Yes, I'm sure." Eliab takes a drink, refreshing himself as a reward for this unexpected labor. He looks to his friend and continues, "I'm not exactly certain *why* He wanted this done, but He said to fill them to the brim so we fill them to the brim." Hand over hand they take turns at this exhausting task. Each pull of the rope brings strain to their already tired muscles. Weary from their labor, they bring the jars to Jesus and nod, too tired to speak.

Jesus says, "Eliab, draw some water with your friends and bring it to the headwaiter." *Jesus wants us to do what?* Eliab asks himself. *Bring this washing water to the headwaiter of a wedding?*

The servers look at each other with fear and trepidation. *This water is for washing, not drinking. If we give the headwaiter this water in the middle of a wedding feast we will be severely punished.*

These thoughts quickly run through their heads, as they try to decide what to do. They exchange glances with one another and they look at Jesus, who, with His eyes, says, "*Go on.*" The servers swallow, and grab a breath of air. Then, with wobbly knees and trembling hands, Eliab dips a cup into the stone jar and brings the cup to the headwaiter.

By this time the wine is finished and the music has come to a dead stop. "What is going on here?" says the bride to the groom.

"I'm not sure; it looks as if one of the servers is bringing something up to the headwaiter. Is this supposed to happen?"

The servers feel every eye on them as they slowly walk up the aisle to the headwaiter, careful not to spill any of the water that they have drawn from the jar. They mop the perspiration off their foreheads as once again they glance back at Jesus. A knowing and loving smile creases His lips and beckons them to "*Go on.*"

Eliab's hand shakes as he gives the water to the headwaiter. What will be the headwaiter's reaction? Will he spit it out? Will he publicly berate the servers right in the middle of the wedding?

They wait and watch nervously as he drinks the water now made wine. The servers take a step back, looking for the nearest place to exit. But wait! Raised eyebrows and a smile appear on the face of the headwaiter.

"Eliab, my friend! Where have you been keeping this?" Eliab straightens up, anxiously searching for Jesus. The headwaiter continues, "Ha, most people serve the best wine first, but you, you have been holding out, haven't you? This is the choicest wine I've ever tasted!"

He drinks again; this time he throws his head back and gulps it. "Everyone, come and enjoy." Eliab and the servers are dumbfounded and joyfully amazed as they look back at Jesus, whose smile becomes their own. The headwaiter again says something about this being the best wine, and the honor of the bride and groom is restored while the music again picks up in a loud and joyful rhythm.

*****

These servers trusted in Jesus and Mary, and I'm sure their lives were never the same again. Because of the miracle, we rarely remember the servers and the faith they showed. I imagine that any act of faith continues to bring a smile to the face of Jesus.

Whenever I read or hear the story of the Wedding at Cana, my thoughts always turn to those unnamed and silent servers, and with Mary's last recorded words in Scripture, "Do whatever He tells you," echoing in the background, I ask myself, "What can I learn and apply from the servers' example?"

The first lesson is to stay close to Mary; as she did for the servers, she'll direct you to Jesus. Her simple and profound words have guided me to listen to and then act on the Word of Jesus as revealed through the Scriptures.

The Church's ancient practice of *lectio divina,* the quiet reading of and reflection on the words of Christ, is but one way that Christ can speak to you. Spending time with Jesus by just reading the Scripture and asking Him to reveal Himself to you can be powerful.

Reflect on a word or phrase from Scripture, let it dwell in you and speak to your heart.

Another lesson learned from the servers is the understanding that Jesus chooses to use you and me in His ministry. He certainly could have performed this miracle all by Himself, but Jesus decided to use others in collaboration and in partnership. Often, I believe people doubt this reality. They think that somehow Jesus acts exclusively on His own, without our assistance. In this miracle the servers are open to being used by Jesus.

I have to ask myself the question: Am I open to participating with Jesus? It's not a question of being worthy, because no one is worthy, but love sees beyond worthiness and seeks to work together. Am I willing to be used by God?

The final lesson, and perhaps the most important, is to act on the Word of God. You don't need a Ph.D. in theology or a degree in public speaking; all that is required is faith, courage, and a willing spirit to let your actions speak for you. The servers did the ridiculous, bringing washing water to the headwaiter, and they saw the miraculous. Their lives were never the same because they did as Christ had commanded.

To what might Jesus be calling you? Healing a broken relationship, forgiving someone, spending time with the poor? Whatever it might be, your life, like those of the servers, will never be the same.

TWO

Above the Roof: The Four Friends of the Paralytic

Mark 2:3-5

They came bringing to him a paralytic carried by four men. Unable to get near Jesus because of the crowd, they opened up the roof above him. After they had broken through, they let down the mat on which the paralytic was lying. When Jesus saw their faith, he said to the paralytic, "Child, your sins are forgiven."

Who were these four men? The Gospel writers give us very little information about them, no names, no dialogue between them. We don't even know their relationship to the paralyzed man or what became of them afterward. One thing that I'm sure of, however, is that their lives were never the same.

*****

"He's home, He's home!" shouted Josiah as he quickly made his way to the home where Jesus was staying. Leaving tattered nets behind on the seashore, others quickly followed. There was still work to be done but that didn't stop the people from coming to investigate Jesus for themselves. The thought ran through their heads: *Can it be true what they're saying about Him?*

Jonathan looked up as he saw Josiah dart by, so he yelled out, "Who is home?"

"Jesus, Jesus has just returned," Josiah said to Jonathan, half out of breath. "Come quickly if you want to see for yourself."

"Jesus the carpenter? Why all the excitement?" *Nobody greets me with a hearty welcome when I come home from a trip or a hard day of work,* he thought to himself. *Anyway, there's work to be completed.*

"Amon," shouted Jonathan to his neighbor, who was walking hurriedly toward the crowded house. "You too? Are you going to see Jesus?"

"Of course. Haven't you heard all that He's been doing the past few days? Are you the only one in Capernaum who hasn't heard the news?"

"I guess so," Jonathan said, holding the fishing net with one hand and scratching his head with the other. "What news?"

Amon continued, "Jesus has been performing miracles, miracles I tell you! Why, it's been reported that He healed Simon's mother-in-law. He also healed a leper with the touch of His hand, and I've heard that He has been teaching and preaching and calling disciples to follow Him. The whole town wants to see for themselves!"

Jonathan looked at the crowd making their way to the house where it was reported that Jesus was teaching. He took a few steps toward the house and was about to join them when suddenly he stopped. A name came to his mind: Reuben.

Reuben, Jonathan thought to himself, *my dear friend Reuben.*

It's not recorded how this man became paralyzed, but one thing was for sure: He had some great friends.

With great enthusiasm, Jonathan dropped his net, wiped his

hands, and headed in the other direction, toward a small village a few hundred yards away. As he looked back he could see others headed for the house where Jesus was staying. Jonathan approached the small cluster of houses and called out to his three friends who were working in the fields together, saying, "Come with me to Reuben's house." He gestured rapidly with his hands, emphasizing the pressing need.

The three workers noticed the urgency and seriousness in Jonathan's voice, so they made their way toward him without hesitation, wondering what was wrong. The three friends went with Jonathan as he told them on the way of what he had heard concerning Jesus. His love for his friend was evident when he said, "Perhaps this Jesus can help Reuben. God knows that everyone else who has tried has failed. I can't find it in my heart to give up hope."

One of the friends interjected, "Jesus, the son of Mary and Joseph? Why, we've known Him and His family for years. An upright man, yes, a capable carpenter, definitely, but a miracle worker?" The words "miracle worker" hung in the air as their pace quickened.

They walked through the stone gate and up to Reuben's house.

"I know what you're thinking," Jonathan continued, for the benefit of his friends and perhaps for himself, before he called out, "How can a carpenter help a paralytic? Well, maybe what they say is true, maybe He is more than a carpenter.

"Reuben, Reuben! It's me, Jonathan. We're going to go on a little trip." The four men entered and greeted Reuben while at the same time moving as one to lift him up and to place him on his traveling mat.

Jonathan's smile spread ear to ear as he bent down to position his friend on the mat. You could sense a little fear and trepidation on Reuben's face, but there was no stopping Jonathan. He was a man on a mission.

"On three we lift," commanded Jonathan. "One, two, three."

The four men lifted the mat as one and set out for Jesus' home. Very little was said among them as they walked; very little needed to be said in the comfortable silence of friends. As they made their way closer to the house, Jonathan's smile slowly disappeared.

"My goodness, look at all these people," Jonathan remarked to his three friends. "Excuse me, excuse me, let us through," he said repeatedly, trying to gain access to Jesus through the front door, but the crowd would not let them near.

Undaunted, Jonathan looked up at the roof, and again his smile spread across his face. He looked at the roof, then to Reuben, and then to the other men. He said softly, "Get the rope. This obstacle won't stop us."

The four men carried Reuben up to the roof and began taking the roof apart. Palm branches were removed until they had made a suitable hole. The four men looked down to see Jesus, who was removing some branches and fallen twigs from His hair. Jesus looked up and a smile came across His face. He took a few steps back and looked up to see what the men would do next. By now, the crowd stared toward the ceiling in anticipation of what was to come.

Slowly and steadily, hand over hand, they lowered the paralytic down through the hole in the roof until he lay right in front of Jesus.

Seeing *their* faith, Jesus said to their friend, "Child, your sins are forgiven."

That statement from Jesus surprised the four friends, as they looked at each other in amazement and then back down to Jesus and their paralyzed friend. They weren't worried about "blasphemy," but were surprised because they saw their friend's dilemma as only the fact that he was paralyzed. Jesus took care of the greater problem first—namely, sin, that broken relationship with God that is more serious than a broken body.

Jesus, knowing the thoughts of the scribes who were present, said to the paralytic, "I say to you, rise, pick up your mat, and go home."

He rose, picked up his mat at once, and went home, in the sight of everyone there. Four men walked to Jesus, carrying a friend on a mat, and five walked home together, arm in arm.

*****

When I read this story or hear it proclaimed I think of Jesus and His power to forgive sin and His desire to bring all people into a relationship with Himself. I think of the miracle performed in a home with the power of just His word. Yet, I must admit, I love to think about these four friends.

These four men thought of their friend who was in need of healing before they thought of themselves. They creatively overcame obstacles to make sure that he was able to see Jesus. What transpired was remembered in the early church and recorded in three Gospels.

In the Scripture that has come down to us these four friends are not recorded as saying a word. Yet I find that their actions provide some of the most powerful and "Christian" witness in all the Gospels. No wonder that the two other synoptic Gospel writers include this story as well.

The paralyzed man showed no sign of apparent faith. Yet Jesus, upon seeing the faith of this man's friends, forgave his sins and then physically healed him. Wouldn't you like to have friends like these? What can the wordless actions of the four friends say to us today?

Why were the people gathered in the home that day? They were there to hear the Word of God. The Word of God attracts people and has the power to build them up spiritually.

I often find myself most "spiritually alive" when spending time with other people, discussing the Scriptures and sharing from their experiences. There is power in hearing another person's story, how the Scripture relates to his or her life, and how this person implements it in his or her circumstances. Insights gained from the Scripture and from others can be life-changing if we are open to them.

Another lesson from the wordless actions of these friends is their thought process. They were thinking not of themselves but rather of their friend who had a need. They didn't have all the answers, but they knew Someone who might.

It can be a terrible burden to think that we have to provide all people with all the answers to life's problems. This does not mean that we should remain ignorant about our faith, our God, and our Church's teaching, but we need to humble ourselves and bring others to Jesus. "We are workers, not master builders, ministers, not messiahs," to quote part of a prayer by Archbishop Oscar Romero that puts our responsibilities in perspective. It can be a source of pride to think that we have all the answers anyway. These friends challenge me in the way I think when I am tempted to put myself first.

This miracle was possible only because these men worked together; they collaborated, they acted as a team. In life we need each other to accomplish God's will. We are not called to go it alone; God calls us in community. We are called to be members of a body.

Throughout Scripture God calls people to work together. From the Hebrew Scriptures to the New Testament, we see collaboration. Jesus sends His disciples out in twos to do ministry, not by themselves. Sometimes I am tempted to try to be the "savior" and solve the problems of the world all by myself, but that cannot and should not be our model. The result of taking on everything alone is usually burnout.

When you are evangelizing, bringing people to Jesus, you will have obstacles. Hopefully you won't have to climb through any roofs, but you may have to break down some walls—walls of ignorance, misunderstanding, prejudices, and past hurts. You may have to creatively use your gifts to bring your witness to others.

The four friends had a problem, and together, innovatively, found a solution. I have been in some situations where I have wished that the solution were as easy as digging through a roof. How do you bring someone to Jesus, especially if that person doesn't want to come, or even believe what you say about Him?

Perhaps you clearly see Jesus as the solution to a person's problems, but he or she may have a distorted image of Christ or Christians. How do you present Christ to someone like this? Hopefully you don't reinforce the image of Christ as somebody weak or wishy-washy.

Have you been using the same tired lines in trying to get someone to church or to a Christian group? What does this person like to do? How can you incorporate your faith and witness to Christ through his or her interests? This can be difficult, indeed, but with the four friends as our example there is always hope.

I like the way these guys acted as intercessors, a go-between linking

the paralyzed man with Christ. What power do we have in intercessory prayer, the ability to raise our friends and loved ones before
the throne of God and pray for them by name? Our prayers are no
different from the work and labor of these friends, and anyone who
is serious about intercessory prayer knows that it is labor. It takes a
listening heart to even know what to pray for.

Finally, I like the way the four friends' faith was revealed by their
actions. They are not mentioned by name and do not say a word,
but what great faith lay behind their actions: a faith that was alive,
a faith that overcame obstacles, a faith that was expressed in love
for a friend.

In my desire to see God after I die, I hope that these four men
will greet me first at the pearly gates and that they, without a word,
will escort me to Jesus.

THREE

Affirming the Stone Movers

John 11:41, 44

"So they took away the stone."
"Untie him and let him go."

J esus asked for help. At first glance this may seem very strange, the idea that Jesus requested help to move a stone. After all, isn't it we who are usually asking Jesus for His help? So often I have overlooked these people who moved the stone away from the front of Lazarus' tomb, and upon reflection I ask myself, Why didn't Jesus move it Himself?

In this miracle story recorded by St. John, Jesus clearly reveals His love, care, and divinity by raising His dear friend Lazarus from the dead. In the midst of this great sign, almost buried within the text, Jesus includes others in two somewhat simple tasks that often go unnoticed. These tasks surround the narrative that culminates in the raising of Jesus' friend, Lazarus, whose name literally means, "God helps."

*****

The town was silent on this warm spring day; soon the Passover would be here. Something, however, was amiss. The usual hustle and bustle of activities had slowed to a snail's pace; friends strode by and just nodded; no words were spoken, because a death had occurred in the village. Even strangers could sense that the mood in the village was gloomy.

This was the time of year when new life abounded and the clean, crisp smell of spring was blossoming everywhere. New growth, another harvest, the cycle of life continued. Not that death was unusual or foreign to the townspeople, but Lazarus was beloved. A young man cut down in the prime of life during springtime. It mattered not how he died; those details didn't matter much to the ones who loved him and to those he loved.

"I can't explain it," said Joseph to Amos as his face turned toward the tomb. "It seems like just the other day Lazarus was walking and talking, full of vigor and health, and now this. I don't understand."

"I know," Amos replied. "Death came quickly for him. My faith in God is not shaken, Joseph, but I do question His timing. Why now? And what worries me more is the care of Martha and Mary, his sisters. No one could care for them like Lazarus."

As the men and women gathered to talk and console one another, people arrived from all over the territory to give comfort to the two sisters. Loud mourning and expressions of grief were displayed throughout the village, a testimony to the man Lazarus. His life had touched those far beyond the village gates. A young girl showed her love for Lazarus by placing wildflowers at the entrance of the tomb.

Jesus heard about the illness of Lazarus by way of a message sent by the sisters. Jesus, full of confidence and in control, assured His disciples that this illness, "[was] not to end in death, but [was] for the glory of God." Yet Jesus delayed for two days; God's timing was not man's timing.

Jesus and His disciples headed back to Judea, toward Bethany, and were greeted by Martha. Jesus told her that He was the "resurrection and the life" and that her brother would rise. Martha replied with a bold statement of faith and trust that Jesus was the Messiah, the Son of God. Jesus asked for Mary, and she came to Him quickly. Mary wept, and Jesus wept. His humanity and divinity poured down His face and onto His cloak.

Jesus headed to the tomb well aware that some of the people present wondered why He was unable to help His friend, whom He loved. Jesus had opened the eyes of a blind man—could He not have done something here for His friend? And the sisters, who would take care of them?

As these thoughts silently went through the heads of some of the townspeople, Jesus made His way to the burial place. He came to the tomb and said, "Take away the stone."

Amos and Joseph were close by and leapt to their feet when they saw Jesus approach and heard Him pronounce those four words. They looked at each other, rolled up their sleeves, and got to work. Amos squatted slightly as he placed his right shoulder against the substantial stone. His legs drove upward as he began to hear the sound of the circular stone moving, scraping against the face of the tomb.

Joseph positioned both hands on the stone, right above Amos' shoulder, and with knees bent and pressing upward, pulled as hard as he could. The two men moved the stone in a matter of seconds; then they wiped their hands on their shirts and stood back as the stench of the dead man's corpse hit them hard. They turned their faces away in revulsion and backed up to quickly grab a breath of fresh air.

Jesus prayed and then called out in a loud voice, "Lazarus, come out!" Dead silence followed as Jesus gazed at the opening of the tomb. Seconds seemed like an eternity as the people waited, anticipating what would happen next. It seemed as if the wind ceased and the birds stopped singing as all of creation awaited the response to those few words.

The eyes of those gathered widened, and mouths opened up in utter amazement as they saw a cloth-bound figure struggle to move forward. It was Lazarus, and he came out.

Lazarus came out!

"Untie him and let him go," were Jesus' words to "them," and they approached Lazarus despite the stench and began to unbind the burial bands in which he was wrapped. They rolled up the bands and cloth together and stepped back. They would not have believed what they had just seen if they had not witnessed it themselves, and even then they were dumbfounded.

*****

A truly amazing miracle by Jesus, the restoring of life to His friend and the return of a brother to his sisters. The image of these men removing the stone and unbinding Lazarus has left an impression on me that I can't shake. I ask myself, Couldn't Jesus have done that Himself? By just saying the word, couldn't Jesus have commanded the stone to be rolled away? Couldn't He, who by His word opened the eyes of the blind and calmed the sea, have moved a simple stone?

I imagine so, but it's as if before the power of God was unleashed through Jesus, He asked for assistance. Silently, and without urging, some person or persons helped remove a stone and unbind a man who was not free. What witness is there for me in their actions?

When I think about that scene and the request of Jesus, I wonder what "stones" He might be asking me to remove before the power of God is unleashed in my own life. These "stones" may come in many shapes and sizes, and we may remove them ourselves or with the help of others, but they prevent us from experiencing the new life that Jesus can give. We must therefore always look at the stones in our own lives first before we go about the business of moving them for others.

What "stones" or impediments may God be calling you to remove? In my own life some of these stones have been attitudes toward others and ignorance of the Scriptures, Church teaching, and, most importantly, sin.

As I grow closer in my walk with Jesus He has a way of pointing out areas in my life where these stones cause me to stumble. Thankfully, He doesn't point them out all at once, so I'm not totally blown away or discouraged. He has also used others, both friends and foes, to help move the "stones" in my life, some of which I never knew were there.

I am reminded of God's desire to move sin from my life before every healing service and at the beginning of every Mass when we begin by confessing our sin. "I confess to Almighty God and to you, my brothers and sisters, that I have sinned ..." There is definitely a connection between confessing from the heart and healing. I can't tell you what "stones" need to be moved away in your own life but God can certainly reveal them to you if you are open and if you ask Him to.

There are many impediments that need to be removed before people can respond to God's call in their lives. How can people respond to God if they have "stones" of ignorance? Perhaps they have no idea that God even exists—can God use us to teach them about His presence?

Can a person read about God in the Bible if he or she is illiterate, another "stone"? Can a person poor and malnourished experience the fullness of life? Stones of hunger and social justice need to be satisfied first before that fullness of life can be experienced.

This is certainly no small or insignificant task. There are many ways that we can help move these "stones" and help unleash the power of God. They may not seem as miraculous as raising a person from the dead, but in God's eyes they are. Raising a person out of despair or loneliness can bring the light of Christ into a dark place. Are you and I up to the challenge?

When we approach our days and our lives with this missionary "stone moving" mind-set, faith becomes exciting because we have a mission. We are helping, like those who helped remove the stone from Lazarus' tomb, to allow Jesus to bring new life. I am confident that God alone can accomplish anything, but throughout Scripture He uses ordinary people to help continue His mission. What a privilege!

The stone had been rolled away, Lazarus had come out, but he was still not totally free. He had to be "unbound." I can certainly relate to Lazarus, who also remains silent throughout this miracle. God has called me out, but in many ways I am still bound and not completely free.

In what areas of your life do you need to be "unbound"? Do you suffer from unrepentant sin, pride, fear of some sort, a mistake that has haunted you through the years, or the notion that God can't use you? Whatever your bonds may be, if you allow God and others who know you well to help in the process of becoming unbound, you will be freed.

We all come to Christ with some baggage, and the good news is that God wants to free us completely from whatever is holding us bound. What a grace to be set free and really live! Whether the problem is emotional, mental, or psychological, God has the ability and desire to set us free.

I would like to say it can all happen in an instant, but some bandages need to be taken off slowly. You have to take it slow, and allow God's pace for your healing.

The process of working together to remove stones is also a working of the Spirit. In the Catholic Church's teaching she calls for us to be involved in ecumenism, dialoguing with other Christian denominations. The purpose of this is not that these other denominations might be absorbed into the Catholic Church, but to begin to understand the call to Christian unity. The process of healing past hurts and divisions is not a simple one, but dialogue brings us together to explore this call to unity.

Moving stones may be a bit painful and difficult, but it is the work to which Jesus calls His Church. There has been great progress made in the area of interreligious dialogue, which calls Catholics into dialogue with Jewish, Muslim, Buddhist, and other non-Christian faiths to foster mutual respect for our traditions. This is a work in progress and is vital for the life of the Church, which views all truth as being from God.

I'm not sure about all the ramifications in my life of removing stones and unbinding. I know, as do my friends and students, that I'm not there yet. However, I do believe that we each play a significant role in the process.

Think of the people in your own life who have removed stones and brought you closer to God. You can do the same for others, regardless of whether they notice or not. I'm not sure Lazarus even thought about who removed the stone, but Jesus knew, and so did they.

In my life I need to have the humility to ask God to call me out of darkness and into His light. I need to accept the insights and care of people around me who can help draw me closer to being the person God is calling me to be. I need to work together with others to start to remove stones in my community.

After all, even when God raised His own Son from the dead, He used angels to move away the stone.

FOUR

An Abrupt Stop: Jairus and a Father's Faith

Luke 8:41-42

And a man named Jairus, an official of the synagogue, came for-
ward. He fell at the feet of Jesus and begged him to come to his
house, because he had an only daughter, about twelve years old,
and she was dying. As he went, the crowds almost crushed him.

Have you ever been in a situation where you knew time was of the essence, where every second counted? Maybe you were headed to an important meeting, or a deadline had to be met. Conceivably, an emergency was at hand, where human life was at stake and quick action had to be taken.

During those times when we are focused on an emergency, the last thing we need is a distraction, an obstacle, or an interruption. We may even be convinced that our priority is, in fact, God's priority. Saving life and being there for a person who is in trouble are certainly situations where we might call on God for His assistance. In this story we are introduced to a man named Jairus, who was confronted with the truth that man's timing is not necessarily God's timing.

*****

"Jairus, Jairus, come quickly with the water, Rebekah is not responding," Hannah cried aloud from her knees, towel over her right shoulder and tears rolling down her red cheeks. Her eyes were swollen; one wondered how many more tears she had within her. The onlookers watched helplessly as the mother and father looked at their little girl lying on the bed totally helpless. Towels lay all around her and were pressed to her forehead as she stared upward at the ceiling.

"Look upon me, answer me, Lord, my God!" prayed Jairus silently, reciting Psalm 13 over and over. For years he had memorized these words, but never before had they had such meaning. His only thoughts now were for his daughter and for his beloved wife, whose grief equaled his own.

Where the illness had come from no one knew, and at this point it was not important. Jairus, kneeling, placed his hand on his daughter's forehead and then rested the back of his hand on his daughter's cheek, then he rose from the bedside where his daughter lay dying and where his wife held vigil to go outside for a breath of air to revive himself.

Jairus walked around in front of his gate. No one dared to speak to him. His head hung down, and he was in a trance; if they had spoken to him he wouldn't have heard them anyway. He kicked the gravel on the ground, not in anger, but out of frustration. It's often more difficult to watch someone you love suffer than to suffer yourself. This was one such time.

It was then that he looked up and saw the crowds anxiously awaiting the return of Jesus. He had heard that Jesus was in the area, but his daughter's welfare had prevented him from listening to this itinerant rabbi who had the reputation for wonder working.

In steadfast determination he made straight for Jesus, forcing himself through the crowds, twisting and turning his exhausted body. The crowd recognized Jairus as the official from the synagogue and gave him way. It seemed as if in a moment Jairus was face-to-face with Jesus.

Falling to his knees with fatigue, desperation, and hope, he begged Jesus to come and help his only daughter. Jesus could tell from the fear reflected in his mumbled and hurried words and the look of desperation on his face that this man was despondent. Jesus reached out His hand, helped Jairus to his feet, and went with him to his house.

The crowd pressed in around them both, and "buzzed" about what was going to happen next. Like wildfire, word spread that Jairus' daughter was gravely ill and Jesus was on His way to help.

Thank you, Lord, thank you, Lord, Jairus repeated to himself. *At last, hope. Please let this man help my daughter, my beautiful daughter.*

Jairus unconsciously pulled on Jesus' arm, which he was holding as he led the way to his house. His pace automatically quickened as the thought of losing his daughter entered his mind. Hope was battling with despair. As with a sunset, there was still a glimmer of light left, a glimmer of hope.

Suddenly and unexpectedly, Jesus stopped.

Jesus said, "Who touched Me?"

Jairus, too, stopped in his tracks. *Who touched me?*

Did Jesus just say what I thought He said?

The disciples verbalized what Jairus, and for that matter, what the crowds were thinking:

"Master, the crowds are pushing and pressing in upon You."

"Someone has touched Me; for I know that power has gone out from Me."

You must be kidding; this is a cruel joke! thought a stunned Jairus as he looked in marvel at Jesus. This was not the type of marvel with which others had looked upon Jesus, for having done the miraculous, but rather the kind of marvel that said, *"What are you doing?"*

As precious minutes passed by, Jesus spoke with a woman who had been ill for twelve years.

Twelve years, thought Jairus, *another few minutes of delay certainly won't kill her, but how about my little girl? Every second is precious!*

As Jesus was affirming this daughter of Israel, a woman from the official's family said, "Your daughter is dead; do not trouble the Teacher any longer."

At these words Jairus' heart sank into a place he never knew existed. The light ceased and night fell, hope extinguished. The words of Job came to his mind, but only as a condemnation of his own lack of faith, "The Lord gives and the Lord takes away. Blessed be the name of the Lord."

These words were of no comfort, however; his faith was not that of Job, but that of a devastated father who was grieving the loss of his precious daughter. What would his life be like? The house would never be the same without the sound of her voice, without her girlish innocence, for she was still only a child. And his wife—the weeping and wailing of the biblical woman Rachel came to mind, the woman who could find no comfort at the loss of her child.

Jairus thought to himself, *Why, Jesus, why? Why did you wait? Why did you not take care of my daughter first? Surely this other woman could have waited; she was not close to death, as was my daughter.*

Jairus turned to go home, but then Jesus spoke, "Do not be afraid; just have faith and she will be saved."

Without a word Jairus followed Jesus. They approached the house and Jesus entered with the child's parents, Peter, James, and John. Jairus and his wife, still in shock from the news of the death, watched in utter amazement as Jesus approached the bed, took the child by the hand, and spoke: "Child, arise!"

What happened next was a miracle: the child arose and ate. A life restored! A family restored! Hope fulfilled.

*****

I have often wondered about Jairus' silence when Jesus stopped. Was he disheartened? Did he have faith that Jesus was in control and knew what He was doing?

We are not told about his state of mind, but we can imagine what he must have been thinking, what we would have thought, had we been in his shoes. I'm certain that many people have been in similar situations where God's timing has been called into question. No situation could replicate an event so serious as the loss of a child, but the timing of God's will and activity in many situations can cause us to question God.

The first fact that interests me in the story of Jairus is that Jesus is interruptible. He took life and death, as well as life's other predicaments, as they came. Without a day planner or organizer, He let God set the agenda for His day.

How often do I miss opportunities to serve others and God because of my schedule? I have to ask myself, while living in the real world with timetables and schedules, if I'm interruptible. I wonder if what I think is most important is the same as what God thinks is most important.

Am I open to the Spirit's leading with the same ease and comfort that Jesus was? Certainly we do have to set priorities and meet deadlines for each day, but are we open and interruptible, as Jesus was? What will matter most when we look back on life? If we have a missionary mind-set we will see our work, schooling, and daily activities as part of God's plan. The old phrase, "Bloom where you are planted," comes to mind.

After this story we find Jesus sending off the twelve on a mission to proclaim the kingdom and heal the sick—a mission that I'm sure He had on His mind when He came back home, before Jairus approached Him. This mission was a turning point for the twelve, yet Jesus postponed their mission for a short time because He was open to the Spirit and to others.

In our often busy and hectic lives, especially for those in "official" ministry positions, there is a pressure to get things done and to show quantitative, measurable results. This model may work in the business world, but as Christians we need to be reminded of what really matters and to be "in tune" with God's priorities. These "priorities of the Spirit" are not always clear-cut in our lives, but I believe that we can reduce the opportunities that are missed. St. Paul reminds the Romans in chapter 12 to "be transformed by the renewal of your mind, that you may discern what is the will of God, what is good and pleasing and perfect."

Discerning the will of God is something that we have to be careful with because we don't want to impose our will on another and then say that it is "God's will." We have an example in Jesus of a life that was focused on putting God and others first—a life that sacrificed for others, spoke out when there was injustice, and, above all, loved. This is indeed a simplistic understanding of Jesus, but by examining and studying Jesus' life and the teachings of the Church we can do a pretty good job in discerning "God's will." I think I would rather make a mistake in being too interruptible than in being too inflexible or rigid.

Many of us have become accustomed to instant satisfaction, with access to cell phones, instant messages on our computers, fax machines, and e-mail, and these can all be good things. Yet is there a danger of putting God on our timetable instead of placing our lives on His? In my life I am often guilty of thinking this way, but then I think of Jairus and I'm reminded of his silence during Jesus' interruption and I ask God not so much to change His timetable but to change my heart and mind. I ask Him to remind me frequently that He's in control, and when I do call this to mind I find myself more relaxed and less stressed. Worry signals in me a lack of trust in God.

Maybe we, too, can learn to be interruptible. A nameless woman suffering from an illness reached out in faith to Jesus and He stopped for her. That made all the difference in her life and in Jairus' life. He and his wife were called to trust that Jesus knew what He was doing. They found out what St. Paul discovered years later, namely, that "all things work for good for those who love God, who are called according to his purpose"(Rom 8:28).

FIVE

Ascending the Sycamore

Luke 19:4-6

So he ran ahead and climbed a sycamore tree in order to see Jesus, who was about to pass that way. When he reached the place, Jesus looked up and said to him, "Zacchaeus, come down quickly, for today I must stay at your house." And he came down quickly and received him with joy.

When I think of God I have a tendency to look up into the sky. I guess it's the way that I've been taught: God is up there, and we're down here.

In reality, of course, God is present everywhere, and nothing escapes His loving gaze. While I'm looking up to see God, He's already looking at me, aware of my presence and desire to see Him. In the story of Zacchaeus, Jesus is the one looking up to see Zacchaeus, and Jesus sees much more than a corrupt tax collector; He sees a son of Abraham, and that will forever change the way Zacchaeus sees himself.

Immediately before the story of Zacchaeus, Luke writes of a blind man who wanted his eyesight. The following event was not much different; Zacchaeus also wanted to see. Although Zacchaeus' eyesight was fine, it appears that his vision of life and how to live it was distorted. Jesus' glance and invitation would have an impact on

Zacchaeus similar to His effect on the blind man, correcting his vision and allowing him to see the truth.

*****

"I can't *stand* him," said Tamar to her friend Joanna as they walked past the booth of the tax collector Zacchaeus. "He's a foul little man, always taking more than his share. In addition he has no shame, for he's taking advantage of us right out here in the open, for all to see."

"I know," replied Joanna. "If it weren't for his partnership with the Romans he would have been beaten and left for dead a long time ago."

"That's for sure," said Tamar, in full agreement with her friend. "My husband and family work hard for what they have. During the dry season we work twice as hard to carve out a living but end up giving half of it to the Romans and Zacchaeus. I hate that man."

Tamar added, "And to think that he's a Jew, one of our own people, it makes me sick."

Emotions ran hot toward tax collectors, since they collaborated with the occupying Romans. It was the tax collectors who did a great deal of the dirty work for the Romans, and this put them at odds with their fellow countrymen.

"Zacchaeus," called out Saul, a fellow tax collector, "How are you this bright and sunny day?"

"Everything is fine, just fine," Zacchaeus said with his usual sarcastic tone of voice. "You know the people try to cheat me, don't you? They think I'm blind to their tricks but I know how they play the game."

Saul replied, "Zacchaeus, we all know that nobody plays the game better than you, and by the looks of your coffers and your house you have done pretty well for yourself."

That brought a slight smile to Zacchaeus' thin lips, for Saul was right, nobody knew how to manipulate both the people and the Romans like Zacchaeus.

Zacchaeus went about his business with the selfishness and callousness that seemed to be the trademark of tax collectors. But he was particularly notorious for his deceitfulness. A physically small man, Zacchaeus tried to make up for his lack of stature and imagined physical inadequacies by bossing others and taking advantage of them.

From an early age Zacchaeus had been unhappy with himself; self-love and self-acceptance had eluded him. He found little in himself to like, so others, too, found little in him to like, and they told him so. Those who were kinder just ignored him.

As a chief tax collector, Zacchaeus had others working for him, and he molded them in his own distasteful image, passing on the tricks and deceptions of the trade while being careful not to divulge all of his secrets and contacts. There is no honor among thieves, it is said, and while Zacchaeus had working relationships, he had no real friends, only money and things to keep him company.

Zacchaeus went about his business as usual that weekday and was walking with a slow, confident stride when suddenly a face appeared before him, smiling ear to ear. Astonished, Zacchaeus said, "Levi, is that you?" (See Lk 5:27-32.)

After a long embrace, Zacchaeus stepped back in utter amazement, scratched his head, and said, "I was wondering what happened to you. The last I heard you had left your tax post one day and never come back. What happened?"

Levi embraced him again and said, "Yes, it's me, my dear friend. My life has taken—how shall I say it—a sudden change of direction."

"What happened, Levi?" asked a still startled Zacchaeus. "Of all the tax collectors with whom I've been associated, you were the one to whom I was closest, and then it seemed that you dropped off the face of the earth without a word to anyone."

"Zacchaeus, let's grab something to eat. You still live in that mansion, don't you?" Levi laughed as he said this and he placed his arm around Zacchaeus' shoulder as they began to walk.

"Something unbelievable has happened in my life and I need to share it with you. I couldn't find the proper words at first but I think I'm ready to tell you."

With piqued curiosity, Zacchaeus invited Levi to sit down as he shared about his encounter with a Jewish rabbi named Jesus.

"Hold it right there, Levi," moaned Zacchaeus as he leaned back in his chair and crossed his arms. And then, even before Levi got out his second thought, he said, "All my life those Pharisees and religious leaders have been giving me a hard time; don't tell me that you, a tax collector, are now attached to one of them."

Levi placed his hands on his knees, looked down briefly, quietly prayed, then looked up at Zacchaeus and continued.

"Zacchaeus, I, of all people, know what you've been through and what it feels like to be a tax collector. I know what it is to have people look at you with hate and disgust. I had almost as much money and as many possessions as you do, but I was dying inside, and I think you are too."

Zacchaeus was struck by the sincerity and frankness of Levi's words. Not many people had earned his respect and could speak to him this way, so in silence he listened as Levi spoke of what had happened to him a while back.

Levi continued, "I was sitting at my customs post, just like every other day, collecting taxes, overcharging people, deceiving the ignorant Romans, and generally hating life. Then, quite unexpectedly, a man named Jesus came over to me and said two words that changed my life.

I'll never forget them. He simply and plainly said, 'Follow Me.'"

Zacchaeus listened intently to this story. What fascinated Zacchaeus more than Levi's words were his old friend's smile and the excitement that permeated his whole being while he was telling of the encounter with Jesus. Something had definitely changed with his friend, and Zacchaeus wanted to know more.

"Follow Me? What did He mean, Levi?"

Levi shook his head with a smile and a laugh and leaned his arms on the table as he answered, "That's what's so amazing. I didn't really know the full extent of what He meant at the time. I just knew that in my heart of hearts I needed to follow this man. I couldn't put my finger on it then, but something inside me drew me toward Him! Zacchaeus, I hungered for a purpose and meaning in life, and this man has given me much more than I ever could have dreamed of. It's amazing."

Zacchaeus was speechless. He knew exactly what Levi was talking about: that hunger inside of him was still alive, wanting life but unable to find it in money or power.

Levi continued, "At first I just thought He meant for me to follow Him to the next town, but the more I got to know Him the more I understood what it means to follow Him every day."

Zacchaeus looked at Levi and knew that his friend possessed something he didn't—a fulfilled heart.

"When can I meet this Jesus?" asked Zacchaeus. "I'm not saying I'm going to follow Him, but I would like to see Him for myself."

"Ah, Zacchaeus, those words make me glad. That's all I ask—that you come and see for yourself. I have heard from a few of His disciples that He is resolved to enter Jerusalem, so that means He will be passing through Jericho. Make sure you see Him when He does."

"I will make it a point to see Him, Levi," said Zacchaeus as they both rose from the table. After one more embrace they parted company and Zacchaeus scratched his head as Levi slowly walked down the road and out of view.

Zacchaeus didn't know exactly what to make of his reunion with Levi. They had similar backgrounds, yet most definitely something had happened in Levi's life that gave him a joy that eluded Zacchaeus.

Not much changed in the ordinary routine of tax collecting for Zacchaeus or in his malevolent demeanor, but nevertheless the words and witness of Levi were slowly churning in his heart.

Not long afterward, news spread that Jesus was approaching Jericho.

"Out of my way," barked an anxious and nervous Zacchaeus as he tried to make his way toward Jesus, who was being mobbed by the crowd.

"Please let me through. I must see Him," said an increasingly frustrated Zacchaeus, as the crowd of people became an impenetrable wall separating him from Jesus. This was the first time in years that Zacchaeus remembered saying the word "please," which even caught him a little off guard. The crowd was unsympathetic when they turned and looked down to see that it was Zacchaeus making all of this fuss.

Zacchaeus' aggravation subsided momentarily as his resourceful and innovative nature kicked into gear. He paused for a moment and then looked down the path that Jesus was taking.

Aha, Zacchaeus said to himself as he noticed a sycamore tree along the path. He ran quickly ahead one hundred yards or so and approached the sycamore tree. It quickly occurred to him that it had been years since he had last climbed a tree or even run.

The thought of his running and climbing a tree was so out of character that it made him raise his eyebrows in near disbelief at what he was about to do. He stood by the sycamore, pondering this momentarily, but something inside quickly put aside those thoughts and he reached up for a branch and began climbing the tree. His soft, uncalloused hands were not accustomed to the rough bark of the tree, and his arms were more comfortable counting money than performing the physical labor involved in climbing.

Luckily for Zacchaeus, the crowd was more focused on the arrival of Jesus than on the spectacle of this wealthy tax collector climbing a tree, and he escaped their attention.

What will He say or do? thought Zacchaeus as he saw Jesus approaching. The crowd pressed in on Jesus as He made his way through the street. People were calling out His name and begging Him to touch them as He passed by.

As Jesus approached the spot where Zacchaeus was, He stopped, shielded His eyes from the sun, and said something which was unbelievable: "Zacchaeus, come down quickly, for today I must stay at your house."

He knows my name, thought a startled Zacchaeus as his jaw almost hit the dusty road. *He knows my name!*

"Come down, Zacchaeus," shouted the crowd, "He's calling you."

Zacchaeus quickly came down from the tree and received Jesus.

The crowd, however, became disgruntled after the initial excitement because Jesus went into Zacchaeus' home.

"What is Jesus doing in *his* house?" they mumbled among themselves. One of them was heard to say, "I thought Jesus was going to publicly scold that dog Zacchaeus for all the times he has betrayed the people, but look, He's sharing a meal with him."

Zacchaeus then stood in front of Jesus and declared that he would give half of his possessions to the poor, and that if he had extorted anything from anyone he would repay it four times over.

*****

Zacchaeus experienced a radical conversion in a very short period of time, and his lifestyle, too, underwent a radical conversion. How can we learn from the actions of Zacchaeus and discover anew the transforming power of an encounter with Jesus?

One of the first clues into the heart of Zacchaeus was that he "was seeking to see who Jesus was." There is often great enthusiasm in people when they first discover Jesus; they devour the Scripture, spend time praying, and seek the wisdom of the Church. Is there a temptation in my journey to stop doing this, to stop seeking Jesus?

Do I think that I have Him all figured out at age eighteen, thirty, forty-five, or seventy? Because I have a degree, have some religious education, or have been a member of a church for years, does that mean I should stop seeking Him? Do I have the attitude of Zacchaeus, who sought Jesus, or has my desire to deepen that relationship with Jesus ceased because I think I know it all?

I must say that the attitude of Zacchaeus challenges me today in my daily walk, because I need to be reminded that this relationship is an ongoing one in which I can always go deeper. Jesus wants to reveal Himself to me in new ways in the same way that friends continue to learn more about each other over time. I have to ask myself if I'm open to seeking Him, if I am willing to grow.

I admire Zacchaeus for his persistence and creativity. He put himself in a position to see Jesus. He overcame his shortcomings and found a way to see Jesus. I'm certain that Jesus did not overlook this act of determination.

I have to ask myself if I go the extra mile and make the effort to seek Him in my own life. It's not always easy, with busy schedules and time commitments, but isn't seeking Jesus a priority worth sacrificing for? Can I creatively make time to see Him? This may mean taking part in a Bible study, joining a prayer group, or performing an act of service.

Perhaps there are ways that I can seek Him during my time in the car, during a work break, or with my family. I don't think that the quantity of time is important; rather, it is the seeking that is key. Zacchaeus took a risk and it paid off in ways I'm sure that he never imagined.

In the past I thought it strange when reading this passage that Jesus invited Himself over to Zacchaeus' house. In retrospect, however, I think Jesus knew what He was doing. The thought of inviting Jesus over to his house would have been unimaginable to Zacchaeus, because of his job and standing in the community. He never would have invited Jesus over, but Jesus took the initiative and made an offer to Zacchaeus, which he did not refuse.

I like it when Jesus says, "I must stay at your house." The idea that Jesus must do anything gives the impression that it was the will of God and not just happenstance that this encounter took place.

Am I open to taking the initiative when sharing my faith? Do I just hope that people will invite me over to hear of my faith and wisdom? Can I be innovative in my dealings with others so as to create an atmosphere where I can, in a nonthreatening manner, share my faith? The situation will be different for each of us, but God has given us the gifts and will also give us the words to share our faith. Are we open to trying it and taking a risk?

Jesus was challenging the view of the crowd by eating with Zacchaeus. By entering Zacchaeus' house, He sent a powerful message as to the meaning of seeking the lost. While Zacchaeus was seeking Jesus, Jesus tells us that He came to seek the lost. What a powerful example for those of us who believe.

Do we avoid sinners, or do we go after them? Christians who avoid sinners miss an important part of what it is to be a follower of Christ—namely, our role as disciple-makers. We are to welcome sinners as Christ did.

Do we, however, cast a doubtful eye on those who are mixing with the nonreligious or non-Christian, as if they were in danger of losing their salvation, or do we encourage them to be the salt of the earth and the light of the world? How are the unchurched or nonbelievers going to hear and see the Good News unless we witness to the faith?

As witnesses, do we let others see even our flaws and imperfections, witnessing that Christ is all about helping us with our shortcomings? Are we witnessing that following Christ does not mean that we are perfect but in a living relationship with God? Or do we live in a world of false piety, pretending that we are perfect and thus scaring unbelievers away like the plague and misrepresenting the Good News and why Jesus came in the first place? Do we send the message that Christians never fail?

Undoubtedly, Christian fellowship and being supported in our faith by other Christians is important, but seek those areas where God is calling you to step out in faith. Imagine what would have happened if no one had ever reached out to you by word or deed.

The text doesn't reveal if there was any pre-evangelization such as that I have written about, with Zacchaeus speaking to Levi, whom Luke writes about in chapter five. Yet I wonder why Zacchaeus was so anxious to see Jesus, if he had not been told about Him. What I have written is pure speculation and conjecture, but I cannot overemphasize the importance of our words and actions as "seeds" that we plant which will bear fruit down the road (see Is 55:10-11).

What wonderful words Jesus speaks at the end of this story: "Today salvation has come to this house because this man, too, is a descendant of Abraham." Salvation comes to us as well through Jesus. Let us seek Him as Zacchaeus did, always ready to be surprised by His goodness and mercy, and knowing that when we look up to seek God that He is by our side, ready to respond.

SIX

Begging for a Touch

Mark 8:22

When they arrived at Bethsaida, they brought to him a blind man and begged him to touch him.

In the story immediately following the healing of the blind man, Simon, soon to be known as Peter, clearly sees who Jesus is: the Messiah. How did Simon come to that conclusion? Mark doesn't tell us. Was it what Peter himself heard from Jesus that led him to belief? Was it possibly what he saw Jesus do? Did others help him in coming to believe? Maybe it was a combination of all of these. In any case, right before Peter's proclamation of faith when he sees who Jesus is, others help bring a blind man to Jesus for His touch.

For a blind man the day doesn't begin with the rising of the sun, it begins with sounds. The sound of the cock crowing, of birds chirping, and of animals stirring and being yoked for work all signal that a new day is dawning. The sounds of conversations between women gathering to go to the well to draw out the day's water indicate that the cycle of life continues.

For a blind man in Bethsaida, the day that Jesus passed through his town would be a day he would never forget. On this day his friends would help him to see Christ.

*****

Another day, thought the blind man to himself as he rose from his night's sleep refreshed. *What will this day bring?*

"Baruch, please move to the right, you're in my way. I need to go to the well," said his mother, Mary, daughter of John. "When I get back I'll fix you breakfast and get you situated."

"All right," he said and then reached for his sandals in the place where he routinely placed them before bedtime. Baruch then reached for his seat, which was always in its place, outside the doorway, three feet to the right.

The day was underway and an older man of the village joined Baruch.

"Ah, Baruch, how are you?" The husky voice was unmistakably that of Uzzi, a wealthy and generous landowner in the village.

"Uzzi, you are always the first one here. I smell the cooked fish. Have you enough for two?"

Uzzi replied, "For a friend, always!" He then paused before adding, "And I also have some for you." The sound of Uzzi's laughter at his own joke echoed down the street.

They continued this way for a while and were soon joined by other older men of the village, who stopped and sat a while before they went about the business of the day.

With the sound of the carts, the smell of the fresh bread, and the voices of those who passed by, Baruch's world came alive.

Suddenly, his ears were attuned to a distant disturbance. It sounded like a crowd was approaching; the raised voices and excitement level grew with each passing second. The smell of dust reached his nose and abruptly and unexpectedly his arm was grabbed and a familiar voice said, "Baruch, rise. Jesus is here; no time to waste."

Baruch was literally pulled up from his seat. If it were not for the familiar voice he would have been completely terrified. Perplexed and disoriented as he was, Baruch was whisked across the village, all the while trusting in the person guiding him. He carefully placed one foot in front of the other, cautious not to stumble along the way, but the man leading him was undeniably in a hurry. Baruch wondered aloud, questioning the urgency of the matter.

"Slow down, slow down, you know I'm blind!"

His friend responded, "I know, I know, but we have no time to waste. Trust me, trust me."

In a whirlwind of disorder and confusion Baruch was brought before the man called Jesus.

"Touch him, touch him please," called the crowd as the blind man stared blankly ahead, unaware of whom he was facing.

Jesus took the blind man by the hand with a firm clasp that gave Baruch confidence and led him outside of the village. He placed spittle on Baruch's eyes and asked him if he saw anything.

The blind man reported seeing people looking like trees and walking. Then Jesus laid His hands on Baruch's eyes a second time, and he could see everything clearly.

*****

Without a word from the blind man, known only by his blindness, his life was forever changed. After an encounter with Jesus he was able to see everything clearly.

This miracle is preceded by a request not from the blind man but from some nameless people in the crowd. Why did they ask for Jesus' touch? Was it because they wanted to see a miracle? Were they concerned for the blind man, or were they just curious about Jesus?

One thing that I find interesting is that the crowd asked for Jesus' touch. They silently took the initiative and brought the blind man to

Jesus. Somebody had to have made the connection between Jesus and healing, and he or she acted, a sign of faith in the power and compassion of Jesus. Not for His word of healing did they beg, but for a touch.

This may seem too simple or straightforward for us today, too easy. We want conferences and workshops and a great deal of dialogue before we begin to decide how to act. We often think we need famous people to guide us when what those around us really need is not someone's dissertation but our kindness, our compassion, and our touch. This is what the man received from Jesus—His touch, not His words.

I often find myself analyzing, explaining, and discussing the reasons and solutions for suffering and tragedy. I think it is part of human nature to try to find answers to these problems, yet the real answer to these questions often comes from a touch of God, as expressed through you and me.

When I reflect on some of the pains and struggles I've experienced in life, I realize that what I needed each time was not facts, figures, Bible verses, or explanations, but a touch, expressed in an embrace, through a card, or through some act of caring. The comfort of knowing that I was not going through this alone made all the difference.

What the blind man needed was not endless conversation about blindness and sight. He knew he was blind; what he needed was a connection with the divine through the touch of Jesus. The people who brought him to Jesus did just that; they let Jesus deal with him. Those who brought him to Jesus didn't have all the answers but they knew Somebody who did. That divine touch is continued through you and me if we are open to being used by God.

Why didn't Jesus just say the word? He had done it that way many times before, why now a touch? Perhaps it's what the blind man could relate to. Jesus, in His divine way, reached out to the man in a way the man could best understand. For the majority of people who do have eyesight, words may be the normal way to communicate. Yet Jesus wanted to relate in a deeper, more personal way by His touch. Humbly, out of sight of the crowd, Jesus did some one-on-one ministry.

What is the message for me today as I consider the people who brought the blind man to Jesus and think about Jesus' touch of healing?

This story first of all challenges me to reach out and not be afraid to touch people where they hurt. Jesus literally touched the man's eyes. Do I have the courage to go out of my comfort zone and touch people where they hurt, to enter their experience and see things from their points of view?

This may mean direct service to the "poor" in my life. If they are financially poor, I can certainly write a check that will help alleviate some needs. Yet I have to ask myself if that's what God is calling me to.

He might be calling me to go to the poor as He did and in some way touch them with my service and presence, as well as allow myself to be touched by them. This can certainly mean reaching out and shaking hands, giving a hug, holding someone's hand as I pray with him or her. It may mean sitting down with a person and giving my time to listen to that person's story and then praying with him or her.

It's true that we can't spread ourselves too thin and be actively involved with every good cause, but I do need to ask myself where God is calling me. Where do I need to roll up my sleeves and touch and allow myself to be touched?

During those times when I have reached out to others I have experienced both approval and rejection. Allowing myself to be vulnerable leaves me open to that possibility. Jesus took that chance and experienced both approval and rejection, and so will we.

I sometimes ask myself what keeps me away from direct service. Is it feelings of inadequacy or a sense that I may not have the right words to say? Do I wish that Fr. So-and-So were here, since he'd have the right words to say? God has placed us right where we are supposed to be, with those we are called to serve in the providence of our everyday lives.

In our story the townspeople were attentive to who was in their presence; they had eyes to see, and brought a man who couldn't see to Jesus. We have the same opportunity. People are still blind to the reality of who Jesus is, and we can play a part in helping them see.

People may come to faith in stages, gradually, like the blind man. It is an exciting process in which you and I can play a part. Together we can help others as others have helped us.

This miracle also helps me to be appreciative of those who have brought me closer to Jesus. Family, friends, youth ministers, catechists, and the like have all played a role in bringing me closer to Christ, and for that I need to give thanks. Who has brought you along in your journey? Maybe you can point to a moment or an individual person, but more likely there are a number of people who have helped you see Jesus along the way.

Did you ever stop to realize that Jesus' face was most likely the first face that the blind man ever clearly saw? By your actions and by your touch people may recognize the face of God in you.

SEVEN

Carrying the Cross

Mark 15:21

They pressed into service a passer-by, Simon, a Cyrenian, who was coming in from the country, the father of Alexander and Rufus, to carry his cross.

Many things we have to do in life are not necessarily our choice. As children we have to obey the rules of our parents and teachers, which will hopefully benefit us in the future but may not always seem appealing at the time. In adolescence, the responsibilities we need to carry out often conflict with what we feel like doing as our taste for independence and autonomy grows.

Even adults, as the stakes get higher, with responsibilities for families, mortgages, and jobs, have to do what we need to do in order to pay the bills and care for a family. It comes as little surprise that we have to obey authorities and make sacrifices for our families. We do not normally think of these tasks as crosses because we choose them for ourselves. Life is full of such crosses that we pick up and bear without fanfare along the way. However, as with Simon, some crosses are forced upon us, and they may be the most difficult of all.

*****

"Another pilgrimage, another Passover in Jerusalem!" exclaimed Simon to his extended family and to those Jews who were traveling with them, their joy bubbling over in song as they prayed Psalm 122, one of the psalms of ascent.

> I rejoiced when they said to me,
> "Let us go to the house of the Lord."
> And now our feet are standing
> within your gates, Jerusalem.

Simon's footsteps were quick and determined; it wouldn't be long until the sun was towering above them in the midmorning sky, making travel exhausting and strenuous. They were on a schedule and were making good time due to their early start. It was a few days' journey to Jerusalem from the North African Roman province of Cyrenaica, and Simon, a faithful follower of the Lord, had made it his mission to be in Jerusalem each Passover as long as he was physically able. This Passover would be no different from the ones before, or so he thought.

"Jacob will be glad to see us," he said to his wife, Sarah, as she kept up the pace. "All the preparations have been made, and I would also like to see Elah before we get to Jerusalem, if we have time. I think we can do some trading with his family."

Sarah also thought it would be nice to see her brother Elah. It had been over a year since she had last seen him, and she had received news that his wife had borne twin boys last summer.

With Jerusalem in sight the caravan stopped just south of the city in Bayt Jala. Those who had accompanied Simon departed to visit family, friends, and loved ones while making sure that the Passover preparations in Jerusalem were indeed finalized. The city looked quiet and peaceful from afar.

Yet Simon knew that this was the busiest time of year for the people in the city. Pilgrims like him had come from all over the world to celebrate the Passover in Jerusalem. The sounds and smells around the temple would bring back memories of Passovers past and give him a connection with his forefathers.

The priests ascended to the temple, while those who sold lambs and doves had their tables set up near the entrance. The moneychangers were still a fixture outside the temple gate, where they were exchanging the image-laden Roman coins for temple coinage. From the wealthiest Sadducee to the lowest beggar, the Passover was a feast that united the Jewish people everywhere. Fear of the Roman soldiers united them as well.

As Simon surveyed the city from afar he noticed an increased presence of Roman soldiers along the city gates and walls. Simon turned to his brother-in-law Elah and inquired, "Is it me, or do I sense more Roman soldiers than usual around the city?"

Elah answered, "You have forgotten about the uprisings and revolts that have taken place over the past few months here in Jerusalem. This is not Cyrenaica, where Jews are in the minority and you would never think of aggravating a Roman soldier or overthrowing the entire lot of them. They see us as a threat, and rightfully so, I might add."

Elah's commentary gave Simon a moment to pause and think.

"I guess I've gotten used to Roman rule and being in the minority," said Simon as he walked over to the well to draw some water for himself. "I can't even think of the last time there was a problem in Cyrenaica between Jews and Romans."

"Those who are in the minority and unarmed are seldom a problem," replied Elah, "but in Jerusalem things are changing. The people are restless and tired of Roman mistreatment and rule."

"You're speaking dangerous words, Elah. They could get you killed."

"I know, Simon. I don't speak them to many people but I'm beginning to see the frustration that our people endure and the viciousness
of the Romans. And after all, aren't you in Jerusalem for the Passover,
where we remember our freedom from Egyptian slavery? I don't call
living under Roman tyranny freedom."

"Elah, you bring me back to reality, which I suppose is a good
thing. But to be quite honest I hope everything goes smoothly and
quietly the next few days and that we can enjoy the Passover and our
families together in peace."

"You're right, my brother-in-law, this talk of politics only gets my
blood running faster anyway. Let's go inside and relax."

After an hour or so of telling stories and laughing and reminiscing,
Simon excused himself and Elah nodded off to sleep. Simon had
longed to visit the temple and pray, so he washed his face and got ready
for the short trip into the city.

*"I raise my eyes toward the mountains. From where will my help come?
My help comes from the Lord, the maker of heaven and earth."* The
words of Psalm 121 were sung reverently and quietly as Simon made
his way out of the country toward Jerusalem. He was oblivious to the
commotion and upheaval that lay ahead. As Simon approached the
city he sensed that something was wrong, that the sounds he was hearing were not that of a celebration and not the regular clamor and commotion of the busy city.

He drew near to see what was going on. A crowd of people lined
the street. Roman soldiers were shouting and pushing people aside.
The wailing of women that pierced the far reaches of the city was
heard. Roman soldiers were leading some men through the streets.
They had crossbeams tied to their shoulders. Each condemned man
had a soldier behind him with a whip in hand to hasten the pace.

One man fell under the weight of the cross, his knees and face bloodied by the fall. The crack of the whip tried to rouse this abject and beaten man but the whip was of no avail. A kick to the midsection also did little to move this bloodied man and only brought more wailing from the women who lined the street. Up ahead another condemned man fell, just the same, but rose under his own power.

"Who are they?" Simon asked aloud, wondering what crime deserved such punishment and public torture. He had known that the Romans could be violent, but now he had come face-to-face with their brutality. He had to look away.

No one answered him. There was too much noise and confusion and the crowd moved as if it had a life of its own.

Then one of the condemned men fell again. The women were calling out his name: "Jesus, Jesus." He lay there powerless on the ground, his strength gone. A Roman soldier turned to the crowd and looked directly at Simon, then grabbed him by the arm and said, "You, get over here! Take this man's cross and follow!"

Petrified with fear, Simon reached down and with both hands picked up the fallen crossbeam, which was itself bloodied. He looked into the eyes of Jesus for a brief second; that brief second of eye contact would last a lifetime.

Seeing the torn skin and fresh wounds of Jesus made Simon nauseous as another shout from the soldier hastened Simon's pace. The fresh wounds of Christ that bloodied the crossbeam bloodied his own hands and garment as he knelt down beside Jesus. Simon wondered what the meaning of the crown of thorns was that wrapped around Jesus' head as the blood poured down upon His face and onto the paved Roman street.

Without hesitation he lifted the crossbeam, placed it on his own shoulders, and followed close behind Jesus through the streets, amidst the shouts of the crowd and the soldiers. Simon's eyes were fixed on

Jesus, following His every move. The weight of the cross and the sound of the crowd were tuned out; everything was happening as if in slow motion.

Simon could see the women crying and opening their mouths with wailing, but he heard no noise. He looked up to his right as the whip, held in a muscular Roman arm, came crashing down on Jesus' back, but it was all in silence. Simon's eyes glanced forward as a hill slowly approached; perspiration formed on his brow. Sweat started to form around his temples, but he was unaware of any of it as his senses momentarily shut down.

They were ordered to stop at the place of the skull, called Golgotha, and the noise returned. Simon was jolted out of his temporary state of suspended reality. As his tense muscles relaxed he dropped the crossbeam that had dug into his shoulder and bruised his back onto the ground in front of him.

The Roman soldier pushed him aside, grabbed Jesus' two arms, and dragged Him to the cross, where another soldier waited with hammer and nails. Simon walked slowly back to the crowd, all the while looking back at Jesus as they nailed Him to the cross. Simon flinched in utter astonishment and incredulity as the hammer rose in the air and crashed down upon the nail head, piercing the wrist of Jesus and the wood of the cross. They did the same with His feet as Jesus screamed out in agony.

A sign had been fastened above His head that read, "The King of the Jews." They raised Him to an upright position, and His helpless body hung bleeding on His deathbed, the cross.

Simon looked into Jesus' eyes, which seemed to reach all the way down to his heart, as he wondered what the crime had been, who this man named Jesus was. After witnessing the crucifixion, Simon staggered back down to his family, mentally and physically exhausted from what he had just witnessed and taken part in. His family, startled by the blood on his garments and by his disheveled appearance, tended to his needs, fixing him a cool drink and cleaning his shoulder wounds. After an hour or so he was able to speak and tell his wife and his sons, Alexander and Rufus, the extraordinary events of the day.

*****

I don't think it was a coincidence that Simon was coming in from the country on that day and at that time. I'd like to believe that God had him in mind when it came to assisting Jesus on His way to crucifixion. Still, I have to grapple with the fact that God allows us to bear crosses in our life, as He allowed His sinless Son to bear His. Crosses that are sometimes forced upon us by hands and powers that don't look like God's. Such was the case with Simon.

The Gospel writers don't reveal whether Simon was a believer, although his sons, Alexander and Rufus, are mentioned elsewhere in Scripture, which may lead us to believe that he was a follower of Jesus. In addition, all three synoptic Gospel writers—Matthew, Mark, and Luke—record this event.

Crosses come to us all, whether we are believers in Jesus Christ or not. There is hardship in every walk of life. Jesus says as much in another way: "But I say to you, love your enemies, and pray for those who persecute you, that you may be children of your heavenly Father, for he makes his sun rise on the bad and the good, and causes rain to fall on the just and the unjust" (Mt 5:44-45).

The question is this: How do we respond to those crosses that we must bear?

Oftentimes we don't choose our crosses, they choose us. The crosses we bear may be God's way of molding us and shaping us for a greater good, and we can look back and reflect upon those times when cross-es made us the person we are today. At other times we may have absolutely no idea why a particular cross came to us that not only affected us but also may have had a profound effect on others in our life as well. Whether or not we see the purpose for our crosses, as believers we must hold firm to the belief that God is with us through-out and that it is His will for us in the providence of our everyday lives.

As Simon silently carried the cross we notice that Jesus, too, was silent. That does not mean that Jesus was unaware. Nothing, in fact, could be further from the truth.

The God Jesus reveals cares so intimately about His flock that He seeks after the lost and He reminds us that even the "hairs on our head are counted"; nothing escapes His loving gaze. Nonetheless, God is silent at times, allowing us to work through the crosses we must bear with the faith and trust that mark the believer.

The scene surrounding the crucifixion was certainly a sad one. It was filled with denial, betrayal, doubt, injustice, false accusations, and suffering. In the midst of this, however, Simon provided a light to this darkness, a glimmer of hope as well as an example for us to follow.

Simon relieved a burden from Jesus' shoulders. What a gift! While Jesus was about to remove the burden of sin from the world, Simon helped to relieve some of the cross' weight from the body of Christ.

Likewise, when we meditate on the fact that Jesus is identified with the body of Christ, the Church, we can begin to see the many oppor-tunities to relieve the suffering that we find daily in the lives of those around us. In doing so we are relieving His sufferings. "Amen, I say to you, whatever you did for one of these least brothers of mine, you did for me" (Mt 25:40).

How can we begin to relieve some of the cross' weight? This begins with a spirit of openness that accepts the crosses from the hand of God and as part of His will. This can be a major roadblock if we don't believe in the absolute providence of God's will in our lives. We can ask ourselves if the cross is something we try to avoid or embrace. With God's grace we can not only embrace the cross but also shoulder it for others, as Simon did.

Simon was pressed into service; he had no choice. There is a difference with those who follow Christ. We are not forced against our will to serve Him through serving others, but as disciples we are compelled because of His Spirit and love that moves in us and directs our lives.

Simon was pressed into service two thousand years ago to carry Jesus' cross. Where is the body of Christ suffering in your life today? Is it in the poor who walk the streets? In a neighbor who has lost a loved one and suffers silently? In a teenager who is trying desperately to find his or her place in the world? In those overburdened by work and the stress of life? When helping others we must be attentive to the Spirit's leading and aware that we are helping God, who often disguises Himself in the poor and marginalized.

Jesus didn't ask to have His cross removed; another noticed that He could no longer carry it. Are we observant of those around us? Most people don't come out and ask for help, and doing so can even be perceived as a sign of weakness that is to be avoided.

How can we creatively help those who suffer, be it physically, emotionally, or spiritually? This is the work of the Church, you and I, in making God's kingdom a reality. It may manifest itself differently in each person's life, according to his or her situation and gifts, but just imagine the good work that we can do as a community.

Helping a person to read, teaching a person new job skills, organizing a food drive, sending a card saying we're there for someone, opening a door, assisting an elderly neighbor, doing an extra chore, are all practical ways that we can carry the cross for another. What other ways can you think of? Who else can you ask to help you?

Whatever ways of lifting the cross there may be, I'm confident that Jesus will say to you, as He most certainly said to Simon at some point, on earth or in heaven, "Thank you for carrying My cross."

EIGHT

Give Us Barabbas

Mark 15:15

So Pilate, wishing to satisfy the crowd, released Barabbas to them and, after he had Jesus scourged, handed him over to be crucified.

Bracing himself for another blow, he pressed himself against the wall of the cold, dark, damp jail cell as Roman soldiers took turns pummeling their calloused and gnarled fists into his face and body. The iron of the shackles and chains dug into his wrists and ankles as he tried unsuccessfully to contort his body away from their fury.

The prisoner's name was Barabbas.

"Take this, you beast!" screamed the soldier Zaius as the back of his hand struck the already swollen face and eyes of the prisoner.

"This is for my comrade Marcus whom you killed in the insurrection," he shouted again as he struck the prisoner's face; the sound of the blow echoed throughout the prison.

Barabbas could hardly lift his pounding head as the soldiers repeated the abuse. His beard, caked with dried blood, bore testimony to the repeated beatings. The room began to spin, and soon Barabbas was unconscious. His head nodded up and down as he came in and out of his dazed state. His senses, too fatigued to respond, finally succumbed to the brutality, and he faded off into a near-comatose state.

"I was sent here to protect Roman interests," reflected Zaius aloud to his fellow soldiers. "I never imagined Marcus would be killed by a religious fanatic. What will I tell his wife? His son?"

*****

The life of Roman soldiers was not easy in the land of Palestine, a desert in the middle of nowhere, important only for the trade route along the coast. Their thoughts were hundreds of miles away, directed toward home, toward family and friends. Life was easier for them, though, than for the Jews who lived in the land and whose territory they occupied, whose lives they made dreadful.

In the most recent uprising it was reported that Barabbas, a revolutionary, who wanted the Romans out of the land, had killed a man, an occupying soldier, most likely. Unfortunately for Barabbas, he was captured.

I can only imagine the torture that the soldiers inflicted upon Barabbas. The Romans, of course, were the inventors of crucifixion.

*****

Awakened by the sound of Roman armor, and swords clanging against the iron bars, Barabbas gained consciousness and the reality of his situation began to sink in. Through blurred vision and a pounding headache he looked up and grabbed a breath, longing for a taste of water that would never come.

Suddenly he heard a crowd outside; the chanting of the crowd was unmistakable. *What are they saying?* he thought to himself as he struggled to hear the words of the crowd through the prison walls.

"Barabbas, Barabbas, we want Barabbas!" shouted the crowd, as inside the prison cell Barabbas lifted his head and smiled.

"They haven't forgotten me," he whispered to himself. "They haven't forgotten."

Within a few seconds of the crowd yelling his name another chant went up from the crowd:

"Crucify him, crucify him!"

As Barabbas sat in his cell, chained like a beast, trying to make sense of his name being chanted followed by the call to "crucify him, crucify him," the feeling of nausea overcame him.

"They want to crucify me," he said despondently.

As soon as the reality of his situation set in he heard the sound of his executioner's approach. The sound of the armor and footsteps were unmistakable. The Roman soldier put the key into the lock of the door while every muscle in Barabbas' body tensed up in the damp, dark cell.

Thoughts of defiance were just a distant memory now, as his strength, emotional and physical, was extinguished. He knew what would happen next: he would be flogged, driven through the streets like a beast, and nailed naked to a cross. Death was inevitable.

Zaius unlocked the door as two Roman sentries, Anin and Dennis, unlocked the chains on Barabbas' feet and hands.

"You're free," barked Dennis. "Now get out of here. I give you my word you'll suffer twice as much if I ever see you again."

Barabbas was frozen, unable to move.

"Get out!" roared Zaius, full of repugnance and disgust. "Do you want me to make you move quicker?"

Barabbas started moving forward but thought this must be a dream. *I'm guilty*, he said to himself. *I know I'm guilty. They caught me and now they set me free? It doesn't make sense.*

These thoughts ran through Barabbas' head, but he kept moving—he was no fool. Despite the unreality of the events that had occurred in the past few minutes, he knew an opportunity when he saw one.

The bright glare of the sunlight blinded him as he walked out of the prison, past the courtyard, and into the street. He raised his hand to cover his eyes but still they burned and teared from the brightness of the sun.

Then he ran, to the point of exhaustion, through the city streets and up the Mount of Olives and toward Bethany.

With every step he shouted, "I'm free, I'm free."

* * * * *

From this point on we hear no more of Barabbas.

I don't like to think that the story of Barabbas ends there, however. While we don't have any further record of his actions recorded in Scripture, he most certainly lived another day. Human nature dictates that at some point Barabbas must have thought, *Why am I free? I'm guilty! It doesn't make sense.*

I wonder whether Barabbas, after cleaning his wounds and washing his face, came back to Jerusalem. Perhaps he was wearing a disguise of some sort so as not to be recognized by the crowd and the Romans.

As he approached Jerusalem, I wonder if he saw those three men who were crucified on the crosses and asked, "Who is that man in the middle?"

"Why, that's Jesus. He took Barabbas' place," would come the reply. "Are you the only one in Jerusalem who doesn't know what's been happening?"

"He took Barabbas' place." The words would echo in the revolutionary's mind as the reality of the situation would begin to sink in. *He took my place!*

I wonder whether Jesus and Barabbas ever made eye contact. Can you imagine Jesus looking across the crowd from the cross and seeing

Barabbas? I wonder what Barabbas was thinking as Jesus was agonizing on the cross; did he ever thank Jesus for taking his place? Did it make a difference in his understanding of who this Jesus was? Was Barabbas a changed person?

I would bet anything that Jesus, if Barabbas did return, communicated this with His eyes: "Barabbas, I love you, too. I took your place and the place of all sinners because of that love. Even though you have a misguided sense of justice and your desire for justice has led you to kill, I love you."

The name "Barabbas" literally means "Son of the Father." You see, Barabbas, too, was a son of the Father, a person beloved of God, just like you and me. St. Paul reminds us that, "God proves his love for us in that while we were still sinners Christ died for us" (Rom 5:8).

We will never know if Barabbas said thanks to Jesus, or if he was changed by Jesus' costly demonstration of love. Maybe he killed again; we don't know. I would hate to think, however, that Barabbas was unchanged by his second chance.

What does this have to do with you and me? Everything! Will we remain unchanged by the death and resurrection of Jesus? Can His sacrifice inspire us to do the same, even for "sinful" people whom we may think are beyond God's reach?

We believe as Christians that Jesus took our place on the cross for our sins, yours and mine. Do we recognize in others that they too are sons and daughters of God?

I wonder how those Roman soldiers felt telling Barabbas the good news that he was free from punishment and free from condemnation. I imagine that they told Barabbas begrudgingly, even with hostility.

Is there anyone in your life or mine whom we might have the opportunity to tell the Good News—but we hold back because of a wrong attitude toward that person? Do we pray for an opening or occasion to share the Good News? Do we feel that we earn our salvation by being good, or do we recognize that it is a gift freely offered by God?

This idea presupposes that we know the Good News, the gospel, and know how to communicate it with words and with our lives. One of the responsibilities of being a member of the Church is to share the Good News. One thing that I have found helpful is to have a one-minute, a three-minute, and an extended witness or testimony in which I can, according to the time I have, share my faith. We don't need to tell our life stories every time we meet somebody, but we can certainly plant seeds of faith as we live in the providence of our daily lives.

We don't know how Barabbas responded, but what about us? Have you ever thanked Jesus for taking your place on that Good Friday?

I find that spending some time alone with the cross or an icon, especially during Lent, can be a powerful way to have "eye contact" with Jesus. You don't even need to say the words out loud, for God knows the intention of your heart. That time with Jesus will pour out into your relations with others. You can certainly respond to Christ on the cross by recognizing Him in the poor and marginalized in your own community.

Jesus' response may be in silence, but in the quiet experience of spending time with Him in prayer and reflection you might very well hear the words of Jesus speaking to your heart, saying, "I love you."

NINE

He Gave All: A Small Boy With Loaves and Fishes

John 6:9

"There is a boy here who has five barley loaves and two fish; but what good are these for so many?"

The miracle of the loaves and fish is one of the few miracles recorded in all four Gospels. In addition, the multiplication miracle is fundamental to understanding the Catholic Church's theology of the Eucharist that has been celebrated by Christians for the past two thousand years.

Of all the miracles attributed to Jesus, this one has fascinated me the most. I have always wondered just how Jesus multiplied the loaves and fish. I can visualize the calming of the storm, I can picture in my mind Jesus walking on water and the raising of Lazarus, but this one perplexes me.

While I struggle with trying to visualize this miracle, I see coming toward Jesus, led by St. Andrew, a lad with a lunch sack containing loaves of barley bread and two fish. Quietly and unassumingly, he gives to Jesus the little he has, which in Jesus' hands turns out to be more than enough.

*****

Passover was just around the corner, and the sounds and fragrances of spring were in the air. The migrant turtledoves were arriving overhead for their nesting and mating season before they continued on their journey toward Africa at the end of the summer. The male's distinctive mating call, *tur-tur-tur,* marked the onset of spring.

The male and female deer that lived separately for most of the year had begun their long and intricate courtship ritual, which would continue on through the springtime and into the summer mating season. The male deer ran toward the female herd and then quickly retreated, repeating this over and over. The female deer did the same, and so began the courtship.

The hawthorn's early spring flower, with its apple-like scent that filled the air, also signaled the appearance of the new season. The everflourishing fig tree put forth its young figs at the same time as the leaves appeared, and the blossoming vines spread their fragrance as their branches extended across the ground.

In the midst of all this activity, Joash, a small lad, was stuck inside, working at a feverish pace to finish his daily chores, all the while keeping one eye on his little sister for his mom.

"Mom, Mom," cried Joash, his voice strained, feebly trying to gain sympathy, "the chores are finished. Can I please go down to the sea now, *please?*" His mother couldn't ignore the plea of her small boy any longer, and the look on his face only reinforced her sense of his yearning to go outside and play under the bright warm sun.

The Sea of Galilee, not more than a half mile away, was a paradise to a small boy full of intrigue and wonder. The sea could hold almost anyone's interest with its rocky, sandy shore and waters full of surprises. It was especially captivating and absorbing for the young, for they were filled with wonder at even the smallest things. Under every rock was an amusement; each wave brought new possibilities for the imaginative.

The chores were completed and it was beautiful outside, but his mother had one more task for Joash to accomplish.

"All right, Joash, I'll let you go and play, but first refill the water bucket and then come to see me." Joash took off like a shot, with the bucket swinging in his small hand; dust was literally raised as he ran down the middle of the street. Neighbors smiled in quiet amusement as they turned their heads to watch the boy run like the wind right by them, as if he were on a desperate mission.

In no time at all the small boy could be seen holding the water bucket with both hands as he made his way back home. His mother laughed to herself as she saw her son walking and sloshing the bucket back and forth, struggling to carry the heavy load as it knocked against his leg. The faster he walked, the more water splashed out of the bucket and onto his clothes and the street, leaving a wet trail from the well to their house. Joash put the bucket down, dried his hands on his shirt, and looked up at his mom with a smile.

"Joash," said his mother, "before you go, take this." His mother had prepared a lunch sack for him of five barley loaves, more than enough for a boy that size to enjoy with his friends. She placed the sack in his outstretched hands and smiled as she watched the joy expressed on his face.

"This is enough for me and my friends!" he exclaimed enthusiastically as he grabbed the fishing net, ran out the door, and disappeared toward the sea. From a distance he turned around and yelled out, "Thanks, Mom!" and then he was gone.

The little boy was absorbed in all that the sea had to offer. The small waves that lapped up on the shore carried white foam and driftwood. Close to the shore, little minnows darted back and forth along the coastline.

Joash took his chances, throwing the net into the sea as he had seen his father and uncle do. After coming up empty the first five or six casts, he felt some tension in the net as he pulled it up. Excitement seized every inch of his body at the possibility of catching a fish all by himself. He gathered the net toward him, and much to his amazement not one but two good-size fish were caught. He had waited for this moment a long time, and he knew just how to prepare them for eating afterward.

A little while later, from the banks of the Galilee, Joash looked up. He heard the loud rumbling of people, a multitude of them. He had been previously preoccupied with a few fish who were swimming back and forth near the shoreline, but he heard the crowd before he saw them and the crowd held more possibilities than the fish at this point.

Joash walked in the direction of the rumbling and saw a mass of people like he had never seen before. He grabbed his pack with the loaves and fish and made his way up the mountainside, negotiating the grassy slope to observe more people than he had seen in his whole lifetime.

As he made his way up to the crest of the mountain he saw a man whose name turned out to be Jesus sitting on the ground, people gathered around Him. The breeze tasseled His long, shoulder-length hair as His disciples gathered around Him. A few men were talking directly to Jesus, and as they shrugged their shoulders and pointed to the multitude, even Joash could figure out that something was amiss. One of Jesus' disciples was overheard asking people if they had brought anything to eat. It seemed as if one of them had asked about a dozen people, all of whom had brought nothing.

Joash walked up to the ridge of the mountain, about a stone's throw from Jesus, and stretched out before the boy were all the people. Joash was amazed at the sheer number of them and wondered why they had all gathered. It was then, while he was eyeing the crowd, that Andrew, one of Jesus' companions, came up to Joash and said, "Lad, will you follow me?"

Joash was surprised and a bit frightened for fear of having done something wrong. But in faith and confidence he went with Andrew to meet Jesus, who seemed to be the one in charge.

Jesus placed His right hand on Joash's head, looked at the boy, and gave him a reassuring smile as He tousled his hair and said, "So, I see you like fishing." Joash nodded and smiled, saying, "Yes, yes, I love it."

Jesus grinned and said, "I like fishing, too. Maybe someday you and I will go fishing with my disciples?"

Jesus then whispered into the boy's ear, "My disciples like to fish, but are not too successful at it." He rose up and asked the boy expectantly, "Will you help Me today?"

"Yes, anything," replied Joash, excited to be involved and included.

Jesus then turned to His disciples and said sternly, "Have the people recline." He received the loaves and fish from the boy's outstretched arms, for Joash had offered them to Jesus.

Word quickly spread from the top of the mountain all the way down to the bottom that they should recline, and that's exactly what the people did.

Jesus looked at the crowd and then looked at the loaves and fish. He reached out His hands toward the boy, who freely gave Him the five loaves of barley bread and two fish; he held back nothing. Jesus took the loaves, gave thanks, and distributed them to the crowd.

It was amazing: every time Jesus pulled his hands out of the sack, anther piece of bread appeared, and this went on for more than an hour. Joash was amazed, as were the people close to Jesus who witnessed this miracle.

When the crowd was satisfied and had eaten their fill, Jesus directed them to collect the leftovers. Twelve wicker baskets were filled full.

The crowd started murmuring among themselves, and word got back to Jesus that they were going to carry Him off to make Him king. Jesus, aware of the murmurings, began to withdraw from the crowd so He could slip away unnoticed. However, before He made His getaway, He looked at the twelve baskets full of leftovers, then looked at Joash, smiled, and said, "Lad, take these home to your family and tell them of God's generosity."

*****

No one can be sure what happened to those leftovers, or how the transaction between Jesus and the boy occurred. But I have often thought of those leftovers and hoped that they didn't go to waste.

I also love the fact that St. Andrew brought the boy to Jesus. Andrew must have been thinking of the food dilemma, too, when he saw the great crowds and the daunting task of trying to feed all those people. In his search he came up a little short. All he could round up was one small boy with a meager amount of food, compared to the need at hand.

This attempt to bring people to Jesus, however, was characteristic of Andrew. (Earlier he had brought his brother, and later on he would introduce some Greek-speaking men to Jesus.) Now Andrew brought this boy to Jesus, and without a word the boy surrendered his meal to Him. What a difference that surrendering made.

I wonder what that boy was thinking as St. Andrew introduced him to Jesus. Was he afraid? Would Jesus turn to him and say, "Is this all you have?" Could the boy sense in St. Andrew's voice that he didn't have much to offer: "What good are these among so many?" I have a feeling that Jesus' very presence put him at ease.

In view of the fact that the Gospel account tells us that it was a lad or small boy who surrendered the loaves and fish, I'm thinking that the lad was excited and even optimistic about being able to give all that he had! He was excited that he was chosen to help, excited that he was included. I don't think that the boy was aware that his small amount of food was inadequate; in fact, I think the boy was excited that he had the opportunity to give all that he had.

I wonder if Jesus said, "Joash, I could use your help." The reality is that Jesus is still asking for help today, looking for an attitude and a generous spirit that gives all and holds nothing back.

This is all conjecture and speculation, of course, but there is a lesson for us, who at times may adapt the attitude and pessimism of those who feel as if they have little to offer or that they can't make a difference. In the eyes of Jesus, what we freely give can make a great difference in the lives of others.

I think of two of our most valuable assets, time and talents. United with Jesus we can certainly make a difference in the lives of others.

In my daily schedule, with all the responsibilities and commitments, can I spend some time encouraging another person, perhaps touching base with that person on the phone or dropping him or her an unexpected letter or e-mail? The fact of the matter is that the little things do make a difference in your life and mine, and they don't necessarily have to take a great deal of time. The question is, however, are we willing to give freely, with the expectation that we can and do make a difference?

This childlike attitude exhibited by the boy speaks to us today, proclaiming through his deeds, that yes, our giving, whatever it may be, can be used by God to be a power for good. This missionary mind-set is not vanity, but truth. It is false humility and an outright lie to be told the opposite, that we can't and don't make a difference. Nothing escapes the loving eyes of God; no act of love is "small" in God's estimation.

The miracle of the loaves and fishes was not a miracle of sharing. Jesus miraculously multiplied those loaves and fish that day near the shore of the Sea of Galilee. Nevertheless, it was precipitated by an act of sharing on behalf of a boy who we can presume willingly gave all. He held nothing back. The Gospel writer records no fear in the lad, only trust.

What is God calling you to give or to give all to? This question is not lightly posed. For if we are serious in our asking, God will answer, and we may not always feel comfortable with what He may be calling us to give.

Is it additional time with a friend or family member? Is it more time spent studying or reading the Bible? Could it be giving more attention to your spiritual life? Is it giving up a harmful attitude, habit, or sin? Only God can convict you of what you may need to give or give all to, but He will make it clear to you, and that, in itself, will be liberating.

I imagine the boy who gave up the loaves and fish probably thought that his giving would mean that he would go hungry that day. What a paradox; I bet he had his fill at the end of the day!

I expect that he told that story until the day he died. I can hear him as an old man saying to his grandchildren, "Did I ever tell you kids about the day I gave my lunch to Jesus? That turned out to be the best thing I ever did!" What will your story be? What will be your legacy?

Imagine if the boy had refused Jesus. In freedom, I'm sure Jesus would have allowed it and let him go on his way; I can't see Jesus forcing the boy to give up his lunch. Love isn't like that, for love freely gives.

The little nameless boy gave freely, in silence, but it is not always so easy to give, because often it involves trust, faith, and a surrendering, a letting go of sorts. I don't think the boy was wondering, "What will I get in return, Jesus?" but too often, I'm ashamed to say, those thoughts pass through my head. What's in it for me, what's the return on my investment?

However, it doesn't take long to realize that nobody outdoes God in generosity when we trust in Him with all our heart. Once we experience the generosity of God we will be looking for opportunities to give and serve not because of what we may receive in return, but rather for the honor and privilege of serving Jesus and being involved in His ministry. That, in and of itself, is reward enough, yet God constantly surprises us with His kindness and charity, often in very unexpected ways.

As a postscript to this story, I note again how I sometimes wonder what happened to those leftovers. I'd like to think it happened as I have written, that Jesus gave the twelve baskets to the little boy and then told him to go home and share the Good News. Jesus can use anyone who is open and available.

Can you picture the face of this little boy's mother as he struggled with the twelve baskets up the street and explained what he had witnessed? That must have been one happy boy.

TEN

His Face Fell

Mark 10:21-22

Jesus, looking at him, loved him and said to him, "You are lacking in one thing. Go, sell what you have, and give to [the] poor and you will have treasure in heaven; then come, follow me." At that statement his face fell, and he went away sad, for he had many possessions.

In the Scriptures are many nameless men and women who are known only by their sin, their ailment, or a brief description: The woman at the well, the blind man, the woman caught in adultery, and the man with the withered hand are just a few. We may feel sorry for some of these people because of their predicament or illness. In this story, however, a man is known by a trait we might be tempted to envy: his wealth.

No doubt many of us would not mind being known as the "rich man," the person with the goods. Even so, few stories in the gospel end as sadly as this one.

*****

It was a good day for Jesus, having just taught His disciples about the childlike nature of the kingdom of God. The parents listened to Him and the children continued to gather around Him, wanting to be "blessed" by Him. The children weren't exactly sure what that meant, but Jesus was welcoming and their parents said He was a "holy" man.

The disciples were a few steps back, smarting a bit from the sharp rebuke they had received from Jesus a few moments earlier. They were still coming to terms with just what it meant to be His followers, His disciples.

Jesus looked over at the disciples as they stared at this "Rabbi Messiah" who welcomed children.

"Come," Jesus said, "the day is still young and I want to make it across the Jordan so we can go up to Jerusalem."

"Yes, Jesus," mumbled the disciples as they looked around at each other, making sure they were all accounted for. "What exactly does it mean to be 'childlike'?" they whispered among themselves, not wanting to appear foolish again in front of Jesus.

Jesus looked at them. He was sitting with His hands on His knees. He smiled and said, "Are we ready, are we all here?"

In the distance, around the village well, a man was scurrying around and inquiring if Jesus was still present.

"Is He still here, the Rabbi Jesus, the Good Teacher? I must see Him at once," the rich man said hurriedly, as if in a panic.

"I think so," came the reply from a child, more interested in the well than in the inquiring man. The child pointed in the direction of the crowd and said, "Over there is where I think I last saw Him."

The man lifted his robe, exposing his legs, and ran straight to Jesus, raising dust all the way. He knelt down in front of Jesus, breathing heavily, and asked Him a question,

"Good Teacher, what must I do to inherit eternal life?" Jesus answered him, "Why do you call Me good? No one is good but God alone" (see Mk 10:17-18).

Jesus then told this man that he should know the commandments, and the man recited a few of them. Well pleased with himself, the man stated that he had kept all of these from his youth.

*****

Up to this point the man had said and done only things worthy of praise. He actively sought out Jesus. He knelt before Him and respectfully addressed Him as Good Teacher. Jesus did not dispute the fact that the man had observed all of the commandments from his youth.

This story should end with another sentence where the rich man follows Jesus and all is well. Everyone would be happy, and Jesus and His disciples could proceed to Jerusalem. The story, however, takes a twist.

Mark records that Jesus, looking at the rich man, loved him and said to him, "You are lacking in one thing. Go, sell what you have, and give to [the] poor and you will have treasure in heaven; then come, follow me" (Mk 10:21).

The loving look of Jesus must have penetrated the interior of this man. Jesus saw beyond his outward obedience and went right to the heart of the matter—namely, what was in the man's heart. I wonder if you or I would like to trade places with this man?

Then, silence. We are told that the man's face fell and he went away sad.

What heartrending and distressing words, "his face fell and he went away sad." The man who had actively sought out Jesus quietly left, for he had many possessions.

Material possessions were and still are considered by some to be a sign of God's favor. Today we call it "prosperity theology," the idea that our material possessions are somehow in direct relation to our relationship with God. The Church rejects this notion quite plainly.

The life of Christ, as well as the lives of the saints down through the ages, clearly reveals that material possessions are not the way God dispenses His favor. Yet why did Jesus, with love, call on this man to sell his possessions? After all, hadn't he followed the commandments?

It would seem that it was not so much a question of possessions as a question of the heart. It reminds me of God calling out to Adam in the Garden of Eden: "The Lord God then called to the man and asked him, 'Where are you?'"(Gn 3:9).

He didn't mean physically, of course, for God always knows where we are. But he was asking, "Where are you in relationship to Me? And where are you in relationship to others?"

Jesus lovingly called this man on the state of his heart. He had the right answers in his head, but his heart was apparently not where it should have been.

What was it that held him back? Was it a specific possession? Wealth is, of course, relative to time and place. In Jesus' day, saying he had many possessions might have meant that he had an extra tunic, or three goats instead of just one. Sadly, without a word, the man walked away from Jesus because something held him back.

We are told that his face fell. I wonder about the face of Jesus and His disciples; did their faces fall a little as well? Was Jesus saddened by the decision?

Imagine all the things Jesus and that man could have accomplished together. The possibilities are endless. We might have known him today by name, recorded in the litany of saints, but no. Imagine the loss to the community, and all the gifts and talents that he could have contributed to the band of disciples. The body of believers would certainly have benefited from his discipleship.

I recall another similar scene where Jesus called on some fishermen to leave everything. He said to them, "Come after me, and I will make you fishers of men." At once they left their nets and followed him (see Mt 4:19-20).

Jesus said this as he began His ministry along the shores of the Sea of Galilee. What a contrast in faith and discipleship between Peter, Andrew, James, John, and this rich man. I can picture the disciples looking dumbfounded at the great catch of fish and then looking at Jesus. In freedom and faith, without a word, they dropped their nets and followed. What a difference that decision made in their lives. The impact of that choice by those fishermen still influences the course of history and the human race.

I have to put myself in the rich man's shoes today and have the courage to ask Jesus, "What must I do to inherit eternal life?" To what is God calling us? We can attend Mass and say prayers and still avoid the question. We can do our religious duty and leave it at that, never confronting ourselves with what God's will for us might be.

I don't think Jesus' question was so much about the man's possessions as it was about the place of his possessions in the heart. The affairs of the heart are almost always difficult, for they call into question what we really believe.

I have found myself striving to follow Christ yet still remaining very much like the rich man; following Jesus while dragging my possessions behind in suitcases and duffle bags—it's not a pretty sight. I wonder how come Jesus is so far ahead of me, and why am I lagging behind?

I find myself trying to reconcile my attachments and possessions with what it means to follow Christ in a culture that advocates the importance of having "stuff." I have endeavored to rationalize my possessions by telling myself that living in the United States in the third millennium means that these things are necessary, that they somehow help to define who I am. But this is a lie.

Thank God that He is patient with me in helping me to realize that it's not essentially a question of possessions but one of where they are in relationship to Him, and if I'm attached to them in such a way, it is unhealthy. After all, a person who has very little can become equally preoccupied with "riches," and this, too, is not healthy.

What is Jesus calling you to do or not do in your situation? Maybe possessions are a hindrance and interfere with your relationship with God and others. Are you working at a job because the money is good, yet failing to do any meaningful work? Are you working long hours to keep your stuff or perhaps to get more stuff, all the while neglecting God?

I cannot tell you what to do, but I have found it helpful to reflect on these questions every once in a while. Perhaps God will call you to be more generous in praise of others, more grateful, or less judgmental. Possibly He may call on you to forgive somebody or to heal a broken relationship. There is still great work that needs to be done in the area of ecumenism and interfaith dialogue.

Is the Spirit challenging you in this way? All these areas and more can hinder our relationship with God. I'm convinced it's not just a "riches" issue.

We all need to take a lesson from the rich man and humbly ask Jesus the same question he did. Then we must ask for the grace to hear the answer, as well as the fortitude to live it out. If we do this we will certainly not walk away with face fallen, but rather we will rejoice in the fact that we are walking by faith in the greatest call there is in life, the call to be a disciple of Jesus Christ.

We need to run to Jesus, kneel, and discern what our mission, our calling, is. We need to let go of those things that may get in the way and ask for the grace to live out our call.

After the man walked away sad, the disciples looked amazed at

Jesus' question. Jesus, no doubt, looked at His disciples with love, for He addressed them as "children." They were beginning to understand.

ELEVEN

In the Manger

Luke 2:6-7, 12, 16

While they were there, the time came for her to have her child, and she gave birth to her firstborn son. She wrapped him in swaddling clothes and laid him in a manger, because there was no room for them in the inn.... [The angel said to the shepherds:] And this will be a sign for you: you will find an infant wrapped in swaddling clothes and lying in a manger.... So they went in haste and found Mary and Joseph, and the infant lying in the manger.

The test results are in; a baby is on the way. It's been confirmed by the doctor and is now eagerly anticipated by the parents, the grandparents, and all the friends of the couple. In a few short months the child will arrive; changes are occurring both inside and outside the womb.

The changes going on inside are without a doubt less stressful than the ones on the outside. Decisions have to be made; doctor appointments scheduled; rooms prepared; safety precautions taken; and a surplus of baby books, magazines, and articles read in anticipation of the blessed arrival.

You can tell a great deal about the love and concern of the parents by observing the preparations made for the arrival of a newborn. Only the best will do; personal sacrifices will be made in order that the child be safe, be healthy, and have all of its needs taken care of. You can detect a hint of fresh paint as you walk into the room a month before the due date, the crib is set up in the corner, and the changing table is already stocked with fresh towels and diapers. Baby powders and lotions stock the shelf below, all in preparation for the big day.

Recently, a number of my friends and family have been having babies, so all this baby preparation is not new to me. I see similar patterns in how they all prepare, as well as in the care with which they prepare for the child. This does convey a great deal of love. They are sending a message to the child even before that child can respond to that love or see where it's coming from.

What does all this have to do with Jesus' birth? I believe that there is a message in the placement of Jesus in the manger, and that it can speak to us today and focus our attention on the manger where He was placed.

The manner in which Jesus was born and placed in a manger was an indication of the humanity as well as the humility in which He would live His whole life. It also sent a message to all who looked upon Him as a child, and foreshadowed who He was and continues to be for the believing community.

Luke mentions the word "manger" three times in chapter two of his Gospel. The manger is central in the Nativity story, more so than the animals and shepherds, for the Nativity scene can exist without them, but not without the manger. We are reminded of the birth of Christ by the mere presence of the manger each Advent leading up to Christmas. Its simplicity is so straightforward that even a child can recognize and understand it.

What can the manger mean to us, not only during Advent, the preparation time before Christmas, but also through the remainder of the year?

In my manger scene at home, which is set up during Advent along with the stockings and the tree, I always make sure that two silent witnesses—the ox and the donkey—are facing the manger. Why? Because the only time we read of a manger in the Hebrew Scriptures is in Isaiah 1:3: "An ox knows its owner, and an ass, its master's manger; but Israel does not know, my people has not understood."

The ox and ass are not very smart animals; intelligence notwithstanding, however, they know their owner and they know where they get their nourishment. A manger is a place from which animals feed, a feeding trough. The idea Isaiah is communicating is that Israel is more dull-witted than these unintelligent animals.

The people of Israel have forgotten their God. The God who fed them throughout their desert experience and sustained them in the wilderness is long forgotten. The people of Israel have abandoned their God and have chosen foreign gods.

With this background from Isaiah in mind, we gain an insight as to the significance of Jesus' being placed in a manger. It is a link to the prophet Isaiah and a sign for all generations.

The inarticulate Christ child can speak volumes by His very presence in the manger. Mary was giving Christ to the world and signaling to us from whence our nourishment was to come. It's truly amazing that Jesus, as an inarticulate little child, had the ability to draw people to Himself. The Magi, or "wise men," recognized Him and were drawn close. He draws us thus today.

The name of the town in which Jesus was born has Eucharistic overtones as well. Bethlehem literally means "house of bread." Jesus, who referred to Himself as the "Bread of Life," was born in the "house of bread."

Placing Jesus in a manger at the beginning of His life was paralleled in one of the last acts in Jesus' life, the Last Supper. At this meal Jesus gave Himself to the world in the form of bread and wine. If we want to be nourished and sustained on our journey we need to be fed at the Eucharistic table. We need to feast and receive Jesus in the Eucharist if we are to abide in Him.

Throughout the Hebrew Scriptures, meals are a powerful and intimate way of communicating hospitality and covenant love. From the placing of Adam and Eve in the Garden of Eden and the instructions to them that they are free to eat of any tree in the garden except the Tree of Knowledge of Good and Evil, to Psalm 23, where the Lord Himself will prepare a table, to the Last Supper, God wants us to feast in intimate fellowship.

It seems that the manger scene is connected to the Eucharist and to every stage of our lives. Jesus came to us as a child, and Mary placed Him in a manger. Were the words of Isaiah in the back of her mind? Was this one of the things that Mary reflected upon in her heart? Can we reflect on what it may mean for our lives?

Where do you look for God? The wise men looked in a backwoods town in one of the most remote places on the earth and found Him. Where will you find Christ this year, this week, today?

He can be found in the predictable places, certainly—Mass, His Word, prayer, and other people—but how about in the unforeseen places and in the unexpected people? Perhaps He is hidden in the inner city, in the slums. Could He be concealed in a room of a hospital, nursing home, or prison? Could Jesus be disguised as a student who is always getting into trouble? Do we recognize Him in the generosity of a wealthy family who donates money anonymously without making a big show of it?

Another question that comes to mind when reflecting on the manger is this: *What's in your manger?* What is it that you look to for strength and sustenance? The world tells us that our manger needs to be full of material things in order for us to be satisfied. Money, fame, position, power, education, and career are what should define us as persons. *If only I had more money, more power, better looks, or whatever, then I would be happy, successful.*

Christians should know better. However, I myself have been guilty of putting too many other things in the manger and leaving little room for Jesus, pushing Him out, as it were. I do not purposefully nudge Him out, but I fall for the propaganda that the world offers daily as to how to live my life.

It is a temptation to substitute things for Christ. He operates on a different timetable from the one I have, one that is often difficult for me to understand. Furthermore, Jesus doesn't cry and scream when I'm pushing Him over and filling His manger with my belongings.

He does, however, let me know that I need to give Him priority. He makes it clear before I ruin myself that He is what's missing in my life. When all those possessions fail to satisfy my deepest desires, He lets me know that He alone is my sustenance and He alone can fill my every desire. It is when I empty myself that I can give all to Him, and then He can become all in me. That shows.

The Nativity is a yearly reminder that all we ever need is Jesus. The liturgical season of Advent prepares us by asking us to reflect on our lives and on what we value as important. We may be tempted to fill even our Advent with shopping worries, cooking worries, relative worries, and so on. It is precisely then that we need to look at Jesus in the manger and say, "Yes, Jesus, You are enough." Those other things are secondary.

This Christmas, when you see the Nativity scene, make sure that not only the ox and the donkey are facing the manger, but also you, yourself. As you do this, pray that I, too, will be facing Him.

TWELVE

Jesus Writes on the Ground

John 8:6

They said this to test him, so that they could have some charge to bring against him. Jesus bent down and began to write on the ground with his finger.

Have you ever had a question that you wanted to ask God? For instance, how did the dinosaurs become extinct? How exactly did the world begin? Is there life on other planets in other solar systems? Maybe you would ask God if a deceased relative was in heaven. Will the Cubs or Red Sox ever win the World Series again?

These questions and countless others may be in our minds as we think about what our question would be. I think I would ask God a less profound question. I'd want to know what Jesus wrote on the ground the day they brought to Him the woman caught in the act of adultery.

When I think of that poor woman—yes, poor, for many reasons— I wonder what she was thinking as she was being led into the temple area. I can imagine that terror, shame, and embarrassment were all circulating in her thoughts. Visions of her own impending death were certainly not far from her mind, either. Forgiveness and mercy were most likely not in her thoughts, yet this was what she experienced when confronted by Jesus, in sharp contrast to the hypocrisy and callousness of the Pharisees and scribes.

Adultery is as familiar today as it was to those who lived during the time of Christ. It was and is, however, a sin, a failure to love as God intended and a breaking of one of the Ten Commandments. I'm quite certain that the woman and her lover were aware of this fact, but it didn't prevent them from committing the sin.

The woman was clearly aware of the sin of adultery, for she did not cry out in protest or claim ignorance of the charge brought against her. Meanwhile, the man was mysteriously absent from the impending trap of the Pharisees and scribes. If anyone did know his whereabouts, he was certainly not held accountable for his part in the adulterous affair.

Jesus, the woman, and the scribes and Pharisees remain silent at different points during this story. Their silence is as intriguing as their words as they interact with one another.

*****

A cool, westerly breeze comes over Jerusalem as the sun sets over the Mount of Olives. The evening meal is finished and the labor of the day is a distant memory. Small groups of men and women gather to talk, plan the next day's events, and gossip, as they have done for ages.

While most people begin to wind down for the evening to prepare for nightfall, gathering up the children and settling the animals, others have different plans that are definitely not virtuous. A married woman takes a lover to her bed. Her sin will bring her close to death—yet in the end she will experience life.

The news travels quickly. The Pharisees and scribes are made aware of the scandal and pay her a visit. Has she been "set up"? After all, they catch her in the very act of adultery. In any case, the injustice is clear, because she alone is brought forward. No doubt the woman is being used by the Pharisees as well as by her adulterous partner.

In righteous indignation the Pharisees and scribes take hold of her, bringing her into the temple area and before Jesus, who was teaching. No one calls the woman by name; her identity is not important to those who accuse her. All they see is a sinner.

*****

What does Jesus see, and what can we learn from His actions?

The Pharisees and scribes used the Law of Moses for their justification in bringing this woman before Jesus and submitting the question of stoning her for her sin. We can only imagine how many times this woman has been used and abused by others and scorned by the religious class.

Was the promise of love used as a lure for the adulterous act? Was it some other "reward" that we are not made aware of? Did the unnamed lover use her and discard her? Had this been the only time she committed this sin? Was she pressured into it? We'll never know the answers to these questions, but the fact remains that she was involved in this adulterous act.

Unquestionably, the inequality and injustice of the situation did not escape the eyes of Jesus. Would He allow her to be used a second time, in this instance by the religious leaders who were fixated on trapping Jesus at her expense? How would he react? We don't have the complete story, but it seems that the details and motivation of the adultery were unimportant to Jesus. He was concerned with mercy and forgiveness.

Imagine what this poor woman was feeling. She was poor because she was cut off from the community and poor because she was made to feel cut off from the loving presence of God, the worst kind of poverty there is.

This woman knew she was guilty, and now she had to confront this "holy man" Jesus publicly. What would He say? Would He go along with the other religious men? Would He, too, make her an example and scorn her? The crowd was wondering what Jesus would say, but instead, it is what He did that is so intriguing.

The Pharisees described her adultery to Jesus and then asked, "So what do you say?" Jesus, in response, bent down and began to write on the ground. This action focused their attention away from the woman, at least for a little while, and focused the accusing and now curious crowd on His writing. It was an ordinary gesture that no doubt surprised and piqued the interest of the religious leaders.

Would Jesus write, "Thou shall not commit adultery"? Would He quote one of the prophets? The woman most likely was illiterate due to the lack of educational opportunities afforded to women, so it wasn't the words that drew her attention, but rather Jesus Himself.

Jesus, who was drawing the scribes' and Pharisees' attention away from her, at least for a few seconds, used this dramatic action as an act of mercy. I'm sure that those few seconds Jesus took to write on the ground must have felt like an eternity. Her life hung in the balance as she waited for the response from the accusatory crowd. Her breath became more pronounced, she covered herself with the scant clothing she had on, and she could feel her heart pounding within her.

At last Jesus straightened up and spoke those familiar and often-quoted words: "Let the one among you who is without sin be the first to throw a stone at her"(Jn 8:7). He then bent down again and continued to write on the ground with His finger, the finger of God writing on the very substance from which man and woman were created.

The response of the crowd was silence. Whatever Jesus wrote on the ground had its desired effect, for they left one by one, beginning with the eldest, without saying a word.

Most people will remain to fight if they are convinced that they are in the right, and some will continue to protest, if only not to "lose face" in front of their friends. These men left in silence. This was remarkable due to the powerful group dynamic present among the men. What a force Jesus must have been!

Such an action left Jesus alone with the unnamed and silent woman. Did Jesus recognize her fear? Was she repentant? Did she have a clue as to what had just happened?

In silence, Jesus and the woman remained. Jesus took the initiative and spoke to her, something not normally done during that time and in that culture. Jesus straightened up and asked her about her accusers' whereabouts: "Woman, where are they? Has no one condemned you?"

She replied, "No one, sir."

Then Jesus said, "Neither do I condemn you. Go, from now on do not sin any more" (see Jn 8:10-11).

Imagine the freedom that this woman experienced after her encounter with Jesus. Those words must have rung in her heart over and over: "Neither do I condemn you." This was a very different encounter than her experience with those scribes and Pharisees, wasn't it?

Those who were aware of her adultery might still view her as an adulteress, but their view was unimportant in light of her encounter with Jesus. As St. Paul reminds us, "So whoever is in Christ is a new creation: the old things have passed away; behold, new things have come" (2 Cor 5:17). What confidence she must have exhibited as she walked, no longer condemned but loved through an act of mercy and forgiveness.

This episode took place on the Temple Mount in Jerusalem, early in the morning. Jesus was sitting in a position of authority, teaching the people. The way to investigate a teacher in Jesus' day was to test him with questions. Jesus' disciples and opponents constantly questioned Him, and this was expected, so we shouldn't think that asking questions was disrespectful. It was the normal way of investigating a teacher's wisdom and knowledge.

This case was different. Here we see more than just inquirers into the teachings of the Torah or Jesus' interpretation of the Law. The scribes and Pharisees were using a woman's life to entrap Jesus. A wrong answer would mean the beginning of the process of stoning, where the witnesses would be the first to throw the stones.

A human life hung in the balance. So what did Jesus do? He wrote on the ground!

What tension must have been in the air! What hostility on the part of the scribes and Pharisees! In the midst of this strain Jesus calmly bent down and wrote on the ground with His finger.

Even in the midst of this injustice, Jesus remained calm. There were times when Jesus would be angry and even knock over some tables, but here He remained unruffled, composed, and in control. What was He writing, and why did He do this?

I'm not sure what He wrote—was it a verse from Scripture, was it a list of the sins of those gathered, or was He just doodling, biding His time? Whatever it was, it took the crowd's attention away from the woman and focused it on Him, on His writing, and possibly on themselves.

The woman must have appreciated this small action if she wasn't still traumatized from being dragged onto the Temple Mount to be stoned to death. I wonder what she thought of this Teacher whom the religious leaders were so intent on trapping. He turned out to be her Savior in more ways than one.

In our quiet encounter with Christ, we, too, can hear His reassuring voice. In the quiet of our hearts we can hear His voice. The woman didn't plead her innocence, for she knew her guilt and knew the punishment. She, like us, relied on the mercy and compassion of God. She didn't try to earn His forgiveness, she didn't make wild promises to get into His good graces, and according to the story she didn't even confess or say she was sorry.

Such is the mercy of God—wanting to be reconciled more than we do. Knowing the fears that keep us from Him, and reaching out to us when we don't have the words but have the desire in our heart for reconciliation. What was broken was not so much a law but a relationship, which the law exposed. Jesus' action is about restoring that broken relationship.

How are we when it comes to the faults of others, perhaps the public airing of people's "dirty laundry"? Our society thrives on the faults of others. Have you ever checked out the headlines in the tabloids while you're in line at the supermarket? There is a whole industry that exploits the failings of others in "tell all" books and magazines.

We may expect the supermarket tabloids to expose people's faults. But look also at the topics of "respectable" newspapers, radio programs, and TV shows. Our society does a great job of condemning others and throwing stones. Despite the "facts" of the story, which can be suspect, most people gobble up the gossip.

When public figures fail, what is the Christian response? Is it the condemnation of the Pharisees or the compassion and forgiveness of Christ?

Do we want others dragged through the streets to be publicly humiliated? Does it make us feel better to despise sinners? Is it somehow gratifying to say, "I'm glad I'm not like that"?

At times, I confess, the answer to all of these questions for me is yes. It is then that I need to remember this encounter and compare my reaction to that of Jesus. It is a challenge to live this out in my daily life.

We all know people who are made vulnerable by their own foolish actions; some are more public than others. (I'm sure we're glad other people don't judge us by our worst sins!) It's tempting to assume the posture of the Pharisees, even attractive at times to reinforce our own "saintliness" in light of others' faults.

Is this what God wants? Is this what Jesus came to teach us? Is this public condemnation what the world thinks Christianity is about? Have we at times been responsible for giving that impression?

Jesus' way of love sets for us a superior example. It calls on the power of the Holy Spirit to help us refrain from passing judgment and condemning others. Jesus not only teaches us this in the Beatitudes; He lives it.

It calls for wisdom to know when to speak and when to remain silent. The sinful woman knew she was wrong, as do most people when they sin. What Jesus was about was forgiveness and restoring the broken relationship so she could get on with her life.

Can we do the same? Will we do the same and leave the condemnation part to God?

Jesus took the initiative with the woman caught in adultery. He distracted the crowd from her sin and challenged them on theirs. Could Jesus be doing the same with us?

Is focusing on the faults and sins of others a way of justifying our own behavior? Is calling attention to others' blunders a defense mechanism that enables us to view ourselves in light of others' actions rather than in terms of the holiness that God is calling us to?

I myself can be a master of defense mechanisms, at deflecting attention away from myself and onto others. Thankfully, Jesus is patient with me. He waits until I focus on Him and His writing. It is then that I come to Him and admit my failings.

In His love, expressed through the sacrament of Reconciliation, I experience His mercy, the outward sign of His forgiveness. In the solemnity of the confessional I can hear His voice forgiving me and reassuring me of His love.

What Jesus wrote on the ground that day is widely speculated upon by scholars but remains unknown. What will you write with your life? Will people walk away from you with a sense of shame, condemnation, and conviction of sin? Most people already feel these things; they don't need further convincing, because they carry the guilt within them. What is missing is an abundance of love, as expressed through forgiveness and mercy, focusing not so much on the sin but on the One who forgives and renews.

There are times when words are needed to direct and instruct people, but silence can communicate at times even more powerfully than words. Let us take the difficult road of Christ and leave the stones by the wayside. Let's pick up the cross instead and follow His way.

THIRTEEN

Judas Directed Them to Christ

John 18:3

So Judas got a band of soldiers and guards from the chief priests and the Pharisees and went there with lanterns, torches, and weapons.

Judas knew the way to Jesus, but he did not know Jesus' way. No one name is more synonymous with betrayal than that of Judas. Tyrants, dictators, thieves, and lovers throughout the ages have committed betrayals, but at the name of Judas they all pale in comparison.

His single act of betrayal follows him throughout the ages, as each new generation learns of his disloyalty and breach of faith. He shared in the ministry of Jesus and was handpicked by Christ Himself. He was present with the other disciples at the miracles and parables, as well as at the first Eucharist. Without a word, however, he sealed his fate and set into motion the passion of Jesus.

*****

"I said grab that torch and take your place up front," roared an annoyed Marcus, a centurion, in restless anger to Tychicus. "Will these religious fanatics ever be satisfied?"

"I think not, Marcus. If they didn't fight each other they wouldn't have anything to do."

Marcus only stared blankly at him; Tychicus' attempt at conversation fell on deaf ears. Marcus was not a man to be messed with; one look at his barrel-like chest, strong biceps, and steely eyes made most women and children run the other way. He wasn't evil per se, but good only at what he was trained to do, namely, torture.

Tychicus laced up both his sandals over the calf, secured his sword, and grabbed the torch. The hours he spent on guard in the temple area were difficult because of the intense desert heat and boredom, but being in the city of Jerusalem and so close to King Herod did have its advantages. Being on guard day and night was not one of them.

Tychicus and the other soldiers lined up behind Marcus and waited.

"What have you been hearing?" one of the soldiers quietly asked Tychicus.

"As far as I can tell it's another religious revolt, perhaps a plot against the Pharisees or Sadducees, who can tell?"

The soldier replied, "I'm not exactly sure myself, but before the Passover there always seems to be trouble."

Then something quite out of the ordinary happened immediately outside of the city gate. A group of Pharisees were deliberating among themselves quite loudly, and then, after a few minutes, they came forward. An ordinary Jewish man emerged from the center of the crowd, dressed rather simply, and went right up to Marcus and said, "Follow me."

Follow me, thought Tychicus. *I have never heard anyone command Marcus before.*

The man's name was Judas. You could tell by his eyes that he was nervous, and he walked quickly, as if he were being watched, negotiating the terrain as he went. They followed him across the Kidron Valley and up the Mount of Olives as he led them to a garden, a place that he had frequented as a follower of Jesus.

Tychicus was right next to Judas up in front, leading the way by the light of his torch in hopes of finding a man who called Himself the Light of the World. No words came from the lips of Judas.

Looking upon them from the city walls, the band of soldiers and guards made quite an impression as they wound their way in the dark of night. While most of the city slept, the light of the torchbearers lit up the evening sky.

As they approached the place where Jesus and His disciples were, Jesus came out to them and said, "Who is it you are looking for?"

They answered Him, "Jesus the Nazarean."

He said to them, "I AM." Judas, His betrayer, was also with them.

At those words the Pharisees fell prostrate at the mention of the Holy Name.

"What are they doing?" asked a voice from behind, for most of the soldiers had their view obstructed.

"It looks like the Pharisees have stumbled and fallen in front of Jesus," an anonymous voice responded back.

Then Simon Peter, a companion of Jesus, unexpectedly drew his sword, struck the high priest's slave's ear, and cut it off. The slave's name was Malchus. Malchus, who was stuck without warning, let out a dreadful scream and fell to the ground, holding his hand to the side of his head, unable to stop the bleeding. Others quickly came to his assistance and placed a ripped tunic against his head.

Marcus quickly stepped forward and with sword drawn made his way toward Simon Peter, but he suddenly stopped as Jesus turned to Peter and said, "Put your sword into its scabbard. Shall I not drink the cup that the Father gave Me?" Then He healed the slave's ear.

Marcus placed his sword back in its scabbard, seized Jesus, had Him bound, and led Him back across the Kidron Valley to Annas.

*****

And so, in silence, Judas forever makes his mark in history by betraying Jesus and leading those who would crucify Him to where He was. This is also the last time Judas is mentioned by the evangelist John.

In the Gospels, Judas never refers to Jesus as "Lord" but only as "teacher," a revealing aspect of the Gospel writers' remembrance of the man. He was, however, an apostle, one who was sent on a mission with the other eleven to spread the word and the news of the kingdom of God. We also learn that he is called "Judas Iscariot," literally, the man from the city of "Kerioth," not a Galilean. It is only Luke who refers to him as a "traitor."

John tells the story of Jesus' arrest with Judas in the lead of a band of "soldiers and guards," complete with lanterns and torches. Can you imagine the soldiers, each carrying a torch, winding their way from Jerusalem across the Kidron Valley up to the garden on the Mount of Olives? It must have been quite a scene to those who witnessed it.

While it was dark outside, we can only imagine what was going on inside the heart and mind of Judas. The darkness of sin unquestionably permeated his heart and mind.

The torchbearers and guards laid their hands on Jesus. What a contrast in touch! Jesus laid His hands on people for healing, forgiveness, and restoring relationships. Here we see the hands being laid on for violence and injustice.

Why the betrayal? Why? At what point did Judas say, "I can't do this anymore, I can't follow Him"? Lay people and theologians have analyzed this question down through the ages.

Was it God's will? Was Judas disillusioned with Jesus' refusal to be a king in the traditional sense? Did greed drive him to his betrayal? These are all good questions.

We can conclude from the other Gospel writers' accounts, and the use of torches and lanterns, that this event took place at night. This is in line with John's prologue concerning light and darkness, which Jesus develops in chapters 3, 8, 9, and 12. In the prologue John states, "the light shines in the darkness, and the darkness has not overcome it" (Jn 1:5). Under the cover of darkness Judas leads the way to Jesus.

How ironic that Judas, the traitor, leads people to Jesus. Not to bring them to the light, but to destroy Him who is the Light of the World. Judas knew the way to Jesus, but he did not know Jesus' way!

After Jesus' arrest He was brought to Annas, to Caiaphas, to Pilate, and then to the cross, and ultimately, after His resurrection, to the Father. In the providence of God's will, Judas played a part in the death of Jesus, and in doing so he secured a place in history.

Judas' story ends in death, but how about ours? Without a word Judas betrayed Jesus. Have there been occasions when we have been guilty of betraying our faith and beliefs? Have we committed the sin of Judas—betrayal, despair, or lack of hope? Have there been times when we have led others astray by our poor example? Have we ever been quite deliberate in leading others astray with our words or by our silence?

Having a light, or a torch, is different from being a light for others to follow. Jesus calls us to be that "light of the world" and not to be ashamed of it.

Perhaps our betrayals are not as well known as Judas', and hopefully they are not on the evening news or in the newspapers for all to see. I wonder, though, if there are times when we would rather be in darkness and refuse to turn on the light.

Do we turn our back on Jesus during those times when we don't understand what God is doing in our lives? Is there a temptation to give up and lose faith when we are in darkness and the way ahead of us seems unclear? We can always be assured of God's saving hand on our lives, but that doesn't mean we will escape the difficulties that life can bring as we live out our faith.

The gospel tells of Jesus' agony in the garden and torment on the cross. This was more than just physical pain—the agony of trying to make sense of a crucifixion, of His friends abandoning Him, of Judas betraying Him, and of God forsaking Him. Jesus was faithful and obedient to the end.

The author of the letter to the Hebrews (12:1-2) says:

Therefore, since we are surrounded by so great a cloud of witnesses, let us rid ourselves of every burden and sin that clings to us and persevere in running the race that lies before us while keeping our eyes fixed on Jesus, the leader and perfecter of faith. For the sake of the joy that lay before him he endured the cross, despising its shame, and has taken his seat at the right of the throne of God.

In our lives, during those times of doubt and wondering what God is doing, we can look to Jesus, who in His faithfulness gives us the example of how to live. We can also look to His mother, Mary, who didn't abandon her son even in the darkest of hours. In the Catholic faith we have the community of saints, who in each generation leave us with examples of heroic trust and faithfulness and who remain alive in Christ.

It can be a difficult thing to do, to be faithful when things aren't going the way we want and we wonder what God is doing. Let us never be afraid to admit our faults and doubts to Christ through prayer and in the sacrament of reconciliation so we can move forward with our lives. During those times when we feel like abandoning the faith or cutting corners with God, let Judas be an example of what not to do.

The story of Judas ends in death, but not so for Jesus. His story ends in life, and so can ours.

FOURTEEN

Mary and Martha

Luke 10:39

She had a sister named Mary [who] sat beside the Lord at his feet listening to him speak.

Mary and Martha shut the gate behind them and pointed to the dirt path that led to David and Dishus' house along the crumbling, shoulder-high wall of the village.

"Thank you," the visitors said simultaneously as Mary and Martha stayed outside for a few seconds before they turned and headed back into the house.

"That's the first good news I've heard in a long time," said Mary to Martha as they cleaned up the plates and bowls from the table.

"Yes, without a doubt," replied Martha, "and they were the first ever to announce this news to us women. The kingdom of God is at hand? What could that mean?"

"I'm not sure, but it certainly was appealing." Mary spoke softly and moved to stand in the doorway as she wiped her hands on her apron and looked out toward the valley. "God's kingdom of justice, peace, and mercy here on earth; that is good news. And to think that we play a part in it ..."

As Mary's voice trailed off, she stood there for a few more seconds, feeling the evening's cool breeze gently touch her face. Then she returned to help Martha.

The next few days were uneventful in the lives of Mary and Martha; household responsibilities didn't give them much leisure time to sit and ponder the words of these men. After talking with the other women early in the morning at the well, however, they discovered that Jesus, a rabbi from Galilee, was the one who had sent the men on their mission the other day, and that He, Jesus, was preaching that the kingdom of God was present.

Then this Jesus showed up at their house. The day had started out pretty much as usual, with the early morning trip to the well and the sifting of wheat in preparation for the next day's bread. But quite suddenly, Mary heard her sister's excited cries. "He's coming, He's coming!" Martha shouted to Mary as she strained to lift the heavy water jar made of stone.

"What are you talking about, Martha? Who's coming?"

Martha's voice seemed energized as she entered the room, half out of breath, mumbling over and over, "He's coming, He's coming."

When she saw Mary, she said, "Jesus, the Rabbi from Galilee, has just entered our village."

"Are you sure it's Him?" Mary questioned.

"Yes, yes, I'm sure. I'm going out to meet Him and invite Him to stay with us for a meal."

Martha approached Jesus. He had a crowd of people gathered around Him, so she was hesitant to speak to Him. She had never spoken publicly to a rabbi before, let alone a rabbi of such fame. She could tell that this man was different; He was receptive to all who were drawing near.

With confidence and determination she raised her head, made straightway toward him, looked him in the eye, and said, "Rabbi, some of Your disciples visited us the other day with the good news of the kingdom of God. You would do both my sister and me great honor if You would dine with us today."

Martha had hardly taken a breath when Jesus smiled and said without hesitation, "Certainly. Let us be on our way."

*****

From this point we are familiar with what will take place—namely, that Mary will sit at Jesus' feet and listen to Him in silence while Martha is burdened with food preparation and serving. Martha, the woman who welcomed Him, will address Jesus as Lord and ask Him to tell Mary to help her. Jesus' reply has been a reminder and a challenge to believers for the past two thousand years:

"Martha, Martha, you are anxious and worried about many things. There is need of only one thing. Mary has chosen the better part and it will not be taken from her."

Mary and Martha: two women whose behavior in the presence of Jesus one day two thousand years ago still evokes powerful feelings for us today. Their actions appear so diametrically opposed, yet is there a person among us who doesn't feel torn at times between active service and quiet listening to Jesus? Our prayer can lead into our work, but quite simply Jesus says that Mary has chosen the better portion.

This is not meant to be a condemnation of Martha by any means, nor do I believe that this is Luke's intention by placing the story where he does. When we examine the layout of Luke's Gospel we see that he places the story of the Good Samaritan right before the story of Mary and Martha. One of the major points in the parable of the Good Samaritan is without a doubt the importance of action and doing. Jesus ends the parable with the words, "Go and do likewise." The Samaritan is praised for his costly actions while the priest and the Levite are held up as examples of what not to do, namely, walk on by.

So, we can unequivocally say that Jesus is about action. He lived the message of the Good Samaritan parable throughout His public ministry.

Yet Jesus was also a man of reflection. In Luke's account alone we see that Jesus "withdrew" from the crowds to pray on at least three separate occasions, one of which occurs immediately after this story.

So, why did Luke feel it necessary to place this story immediately after the Good Samaritan parable and before the teaching of the Our Father prayer?

I think Luke wanted to communicate the importance that Jesus placed on both doing and not doing, on both action and contemplation. Now, I'm not suggesting that listening to Jesus or praying is "not doing" in the sense that it's not meaningful or even that it's easy. However, we often find ourselves divided into these two camps, emphasizing one over the other instead of allowing one to lead into the other.

Do you identify more with Martha, who makes the invitation and then complains that she is overburdened? (She doesn't even go to Mary with her complaint, but straight to Jesus. I wonder how that made Mary feel? Did Martha carry over her hurt feeling into the next day?) Often those of us in ministry need to adopt the attitude and work ethic of Martha, full of energy and drive, working to get things done.

Or do you identify more with Mary, who sits at the feet of Jesus, listening to Him? (How did Mary feel? Jesus was there in the flesh and Martha was concerned with what, pots and pans? Give me a break!) There is always work to be done, but how often do you find time to sit at the Lord's feet and just be still? Surely this is where it is all at, being in the presence of the Lord.

We need people like Martha in our world in order to get things done. We also need people like Mary to give strength, direction, and meaning to what we do. The tension is to integrate the best of both into our lives in order to be effective with the gifts God has given us.

Have you found that balance between Martha and Mary in your life?

By placing these two stories side by side, Luke may be telling us that we need the best of both Martha and Mary. From my observations it seems that most of us are more like Martha, worried about many things. If we happen to find some time here or there, we will pray or maybe in lip service offer up our busy schedule and unite it with Christ. Finding time, or, more importantly, making time to sit at Jesus' feet is what the example of Mary calls us to. This is what Jesus says is the better part.

This is as necessary as any act of charity we do for another. In sitting at Jesus' feet we find the strength of the Spirit that leads us to action. Without listening to Jesus in prayer we will be in danger of wasting time on things that may not be really important. We may find ourselves failing to see Christ in people and in the little things when we are too busy. We will definitely experience some form of the burnout that accompanies many people in ministry positions, and we may miss the more important things when we don't have that balance.

How do you sit at the Lord's feet today? How do you listen to God speak? The first step is to set aside some time where you will be undisturbed and uninterrupted. The fact that you have a desire to pray and "sit at His feet" is a sign that God is active and moving in your life already, and that pleases Him.

Don't feel you need to be a Martha in prayer! Don't feel like you even have to do anything; Mary sat and listened, and so can you. The same Jesus who was present to her is present to you as well.

I've found it helpful to focus on a word or biblical name of God during these quiet times. Let God speak to your heart through that word. At other times I have found focusing on an icon can be a powerful way to allow God to speak to me.

Spending time with Jesus in Eucharistic adoration is yet another way that God speaks to the heart. I also love opening up the Scripture and letting God speak to me through His Word, the ancient practice of *lectio divina*.

Another way of listening to Jesus involves others. I have gained fantastic insights from others that have profoundly influenced my understanding of Jesus' words in Scripture. Breaking open the Scripture in a Bible study opens us up to the experiences of others and can cause us to reflect on our own experiences. Studying the Bible with others can also trigger in us new ways of applying the Scripture that we may not have thought of.

It is interesting to remember that Mary took the position of a student at Jesus' feet while He taught. Jesus allowed a woman to assume the position of a student in a society that didn't grant women that privilege. Jesus is truly open to all people who approach Him with a desire to learn from Him.

Many formal Scripture classes and certificate programs in Catholic colleges, universities, and seminaries are open to lay students interested in studying the Scriptures. Many churches offer weekly Bible studies for the purpose of providing a relaxed atmosphere and helpful approaches to studying the Bible with others. There are also many pamphlets and Scripture study guides that can help us get into the Bible.

It may be intimidating for you to join a group if you feel that you don't know much about the Bible. But what better way to start? All of us were there at some point in our lives; you may be surprised how much you do know.

Let us consider Mary's example of quiet contemplation of our Lord's words. Looking back with the hindsight of two thousand years, you can ask yourself this question: Who chose the better part that day, Martha or Mary?

Let us follow Mary's example as she followed Him, in silence.

FIFTEEN

Mary at the Cross

John 19:25-27

Standing by the cross of Jesus were his mother and his mother's sister, Mary the wife of Clopas, and Mary of Magdala. When Jesus saw his mother and the disciple there whom he loved, he said to his mother, "Woman, behold, your son." Then he said to the disciple, "Behold, your mother." And from that hour the disciple took her into his home.

O f all the figures in the Bible, Mary stands out as the great woman of faith. Her yes in response to God's call set into motion a salvation for all of us. She is the one who is "blessed among women."

Additionally, one would struggle to find a more significant person who says much less in the Gospels. Hers is a silent yet potent witness. Mary does not need a multitude of words.

Without a word Mary stood by her son during the crucifixion. Mary witnessed Jesus' agony, His pain, and His death. Jesus witnessed her agony as well, the agony of a mother unable to assist her only son as He was unjustly condemned and crucified. At first glance it seems as though they were able to do little to help ease each other's pain. Nevertheless, Jesus and Mary did all that they could, and that was enough.

*****

The soldiers had just hammered the nail through the hand of Jesus. His scream of agony didn't bother them, for they had done this before, too many times to count. If they had looked at the convicted man, they would have found the task more difficult, so they cast their eyes at the tools with which this crucified man had once made his living—a hammer and some nails. Jesus was crucified along with two others that day in Jerusalem, as recorded in the Scriptures, but the Roman soldiers who nailed Him to the cross had some unfinished business to attend to that day.

"One for each, one for each," shouted Demetrius as he turned to Titus, holding up a piece of Jesus' clothing.

"This will do nicely for me; get your own, Patrobus," yelled Titus to his countryman, who was grabbing the edge of the garment he was holding.

"All right, all right, this one is mine."

In the midst of the wailing from those around the cross and the jeering of the crowd, the soldiers were preoccupied with getting something for themselves, as their greed dictated.

"That tunic is mine. Hands off," voiced Demetrius, the oldest and the surliest of the group.

"No way, Demetrius, you may be the oldest but that does not entitle you to the tunic. That would bring a very nice price at the market."

The three soldiers stood before Demetrius, unyielding in their position. He knew that he wouldn't get away with it, but he also knew that it would be a shame to tear the seamless garment, so he offered a solution. "Let's cast lots for it. That way it will remain in one piece."

They all agreed and the gambling began.

In the shadow of the cross, amongst the commotion of the soldiers, the Pharisees arguing over the placard placed above Jesus' head with the inscription, "The King of the Jews," and the crowd of spectators stood Mary, ever faithful.

At the foot of the cross, aware of the soldiers gambling for her son's last possessions on Earth, she stood watching, recalling the words of the prophetess Anna and the righteous man Simeon that had been spoken so many years ago in Jerusalem in the temple. Some thirty-odd years ago life had stretched out before the child Jesus; now He was stretched out on a cross, preparing for death.

A sword was passing through Mary's heart, more agonizing than any physical pain she could imagine. No words passed her blessed lips; no words needed to. She gazed upward at her son.

Nailed to the wood, He pressed up on the nail piercing His feet to grab a breath of air before tilting His head to the side to glimpse the face of His mother. Their eyes met. Jesus exhaled and slumped down, feeling the pressure and weight of His own body on the nails in His hands.

The sound of the crowd faded in and out, and the bloodied Christ struggled to focus. Again He pressed down to straighten His legs, and He looked at Mary, who was now embraced by John. Jesus said, "Woman, behold, your son." Then He said to the disciple, "Behold, your mother."

"I thirst."

"It is finished."

*****

It can be much more painful to watch someone you love suffer than to suffer yourself. Mary knew this truth; she lived it.

Other people, too, mothers and fathers, family and friends have been witness to suffering. Our world is full of suffering. No one escapes its touch. We do, however, have a choice as to how to respond to it.

What can we learn from Mary and her wordless witness? One of the lessons from Mary's presence at the cross is the importance of being there when and where there is suffering. The value and significance of presence must never be underestimated. In modern times men and women such as Mother Teresa, St. Maximillian Kolbe, Dorothy Day, Father Thomas Judge, and Father Dennis Berry have responded heroically to the cry of the poor and the suffering.

What does it take to be present for others in our lives? A person must first realize that another is suffering in order to be there. Often I am so concerned about my own affairs that I may miss the suffering of another. I need to ask God continually for a sensitive spirit that is aware of the lives of those around me, especially those whom God has called close to me.

Nothing could have stopped Mary from being there, from giving support to Jesus. He was, of course, her son.

I would venture to guess that Mary wasn't thinking "theologically" at the cross. She wasn't trying to figure out how this grave injustice fit into God's "master plan" or to tell herself that she wasn't upset because this was obviously God's will. I'm certain Mary and St. John didn't have a picnic because they knew it would all turn out for the best. St. John wasn't callous enough to say to Mary, "Stop worrying and shape up!" and then start quoting verses from Scripture during her time at the cross. No, in silence they waited and gave comfort by their presence.

We need to allow others to grieve at their own pace; everyone is different and has a different timetable. Just because we dealt with a loss in a six-month period doesn't mean others will. We need to ask, "How can I serve you best during this time of suffering?" Maybe just asking the question will be enough for the person who is suffering.

There is a great temptation to want to speak during times of trial and duress. We somehow feel that we are supposed to say something, some magic words to make everything OK. Yet the little we do say is rarely remembered by those who are suffering. What is remembered is that we were there; we offered a hug, our phone number, our presence. We brought over some food, or a candle. We sat with the suffering one and fixed an omelet or some coffee, and allowed him or her to cry.

Mary was a true disciple; she didn't abandon Jesus at His most trying moment. There may be times when we are tempted to flee from Christ and distance ourselves from Him because it's too tough to be faithful. At those times we can look to Mary, who stayed the course and finished the race.

Is there a person in your life who may be battling an illness or addiction? Are you finding it hard to stay with this person? Are you struggling with issues of faith? Do you feel like you want to abandon your faith because life isn't making sense right now and those warm fuzzies you once had are long gone? At these times remember Mary and her faithfulness at the cross.

Mary was not alone at the cross; she was with friends. Mary, the wife of Clopas, Mary of Magdala, and St. John were at her side. They were supporting their friend Mary who was witnessing a horrific scene.

Do we, like Mary, allow others to share the anguish and torment in our lives, or do we take the suffering we experience all on ourselves? Sometimes it's not the burdens we carry but rather how we carry them that makes all the difference. After all, we weren't designed to carry all life's burdens by ourselves.

In a way I'm suggesting that Mary had a support group.

In the Acts of the Apostles we find her gathered with the apostles, praying in the Upper Room.

It is an awful experience to witness a person who won't be comforted, who won't allow others to be part of his or her life. A support network does not appear all at once, but is rather a result of fostering friendships and relationships along life's way. I would speculate that those who do have support manage much better than those who do not. Mary must have fostered relationships with these other disciples while on the way with Jesus, and they were there for her as well as for Jesus.

Jesus, in the midst of His own agony and suffering, was thinking of how to care for His mom. He gave her to the disciple who is a model for us all: "Woman, behold, your son." Then He said to the disciple, "Behold, your mother."

In the Church's teaching, Mary is mother for us all. What a gift Jesus leaves the Church!

Mary silently stood by her son while He was on the cross; what words would have been sufficient, anyway? In our struggle to follow Christ, do we follow the example of Mary, who was faithful and stead-fast even at the cross? When words don't suffice, do our actions speak for us?

When we look at Mary standing by Jesus we are comforted by the truth that presence can speak more eloquently than words. This is also a part of the mystery of praying the rosary. While meditating on the life of Christ we are called to enter into His life and the life experience of Mary. Throughout the joyful, sorrowful, and glorious mysteries we have an opportunity to reflect on our own experiences and unite them to Jesus and to Mary.

Oftentimes to the outsider, praying the rosary may seem strange. "What is the fingering of the beads and the recitation of all those 'Hail Marys really about?" they may ask. "I don't see that in the Scripture."

It takes the actual praying of the rosary to begin to understand it. My experience has been that the time spent in quiet contemplation of the life of Jesus through the rosary leads to a deepening of the interior spiritual life. The rosary leads us to Jesus, which is the desire of Mary.

There is a time and a place for words; indeed, they can help to heal wounds and give comfort and hope. Yet silence can be just as powerful. Your presence at the side of a loved one, at a child's ball game, at a music recital, or at the dinner table and at the Eucharistic table is also a powerful witness. Never be afraid to stand with the suffering, for whatever we do to the least of these, our brothers and sisters, we do for Him.

SIXTEEN

Offering Gifts to the King of the Jews

Matthew 2:10-11

They were overjoyed at seeing the star, and on entering the house they saw the child with Mary his mother. They prostrated themselves and did him homage. Then they opened their treasures and offered him gifts of gold, frankincense, and myrrh.

What Christmas Nativity scene would be complete without the Magi kneeling at the manger of Jesus with gifts in hand? They have been depicted in paintings, song, sculpture, mosaics, and stained glass throughout the ages. Right there at the foot of the manger with St. Joseph and Mary, they pay Jesus homage and offer their gifts to Him.

In this passage from Matthew's Gospel we can picture these strange visitors arriving from the East, gazing above, seeking guidance from the star. It is they who first gave Jesus the title "King of the Jews" (Mt 2:2). These gentiles were the first to seek after the newborn.

They set foot into the village and entered the house. Without a word, Mary and St. Joseph witnessed this strange event and showed them hospitality. What were Mary and St. Joseph thinking? Luke tells us that Mary reflected upon these things in her heart, and I'm sure St. Joseph did the same, but what of these Magi, these wise men? What could God be saying to us through their silence?

*****

"King Herod, may I see you in private? I think you'll find the information I have very interesting," said Archelaus, one of Herod's sons.

"You may tell me here and now," barked an angry Herod, for he trusted no one, least of all his sons.

"All right, Father, I have received word that there are some visitors from the East, Persia I believe, who are making their way through Jerusalem inquiring about the newborn 'King of the Jews.' They are starting to stir some of the people and I thought you should know about it before the news spreads and troubles the people more than usual."

"King of the Jews?" responded Herod as he sat slouched on his throne, half irritated and half paranoid about having his kingdom threatened. "Did you say a 'newborn'?"

"That's the news my informers have just disclosed to me, Father. I thought you should be informed as soon as possible."

"Well done, Archelaus. I may have underestimated you in the past but now I recognize that you truly have my best interest in mind."

"As always, Father," replied Archelaus, pleased with himself and the trust that he had earned from his father.

Herod then asked one of his subordinates, his chief in command, "So what do we do now with these men from the East?"

"Your army could easily capture them and have them killed. I could see to it myself."

Archelaus interrupted, "I think that would be unwise, Father. Let's first find out where this newborn 'King' is and have these men from the East lead us to Him. Then we will kill all of them, leaving no one to threaten your kingdom."

"Well done, Son. You're beginning to think a lot like me. That is what we will do. Send them an invitation from me. They won't decline, and we'll have them give us the information we need."

The unassuming Magi accepted the invitation. They met with King Herod in his palace as they feasted on choice foods and quite openly told him of the news of the star and the birth of the Messiah in Bethlehem. After the secret meeting with Herod they went in search of the newborn King.

Their journey had been a long and tiring one, but they were filled with joy as they set out and saw the star rise and set over the child's birthplace.

The men looked at each other, each holding a gift foreshadowing the fate of this child. "Could this be the place?" one of them said in disbelief. "Bethlehem is out of the way as it is, but this place is no more than a stable."

"Quite a contrast to Herod's palace," said another, "but that notwithstanding, this is where the star has directed us."

They paused to take in the scene. It appeared to be a small, humble village. A cool evening breeze rose up and refreshed their faces. They looked up and saw the star and then in silence they looked at each other. After a moment one of them said, "It's not the place but the person we're honoring, let's not forget that."

After many days and long hours of travel they had finally reached their destination. They looked at each other and entered the house. The first person they saw as they entered was Mary, holding the baby Jesus in her lap, gazing into His eyes.

Mary showed no fear as the strangers approached, only wonder. They immediately prostrated themselves before the child as Mary sat there in silence. She turned the baby Jesus in their direction and she smiled, as these strangely attired men remained prostrate before the child.

In reverent silence they raised themselves to their knees and turned to present the gifts they had brought. They offered their gifts of gold, frankincense, and myrrh at the feet of Jesus in the presence of Mary. Mary, too, was silent as the peculiar gifts were brought out and placed before them. The men rose to their feet and bowed as they walked backward out of the house, overjoyed at the privilege and honor of presenting the newborn King with their individual gifts.

*****

In a dream they were warned not to return to Herod, so they departed to their own country by another way, and we never hear from them again.

I find it interesting that the person who directed the Magi, or "wise men," as they're popularly known in song and writings, to go see the child Jesus was Herod, a man known for brutality and murder. Herod actually sent the Magi to Bethlehem to find the newborn King, who was in reality the King of Kings. These visitors from the East, gentiles nonetheless, bore witness to this great event.

I wonder if these visitors realized the significance of the One they were seeing. Looking back two thousand years later we know the impact Jesus Christ had and still has on the world. But I don't think these visitors or anyone living at the time of Jesus' birth could ever have imagined the impact Jesus would have, although they seem to have realized that Jesus was like no other.

Life is like that, though. Often we experience profound events without realizing until later how significant those events really were. It could be the last time that we had dinner with a relative who would soon pass away. It might be a victory party with friends after an athletic event, which, looking back, years later, we realize was a part of the "glory days."

These visitors gathered silently, for they did know someone special was at hand. After they arrived, their first act was to kneel, a profound outward expression of reverence and worship. Without a word their body language revealed what was in their hearts.

They then brought out their gifts and presented them to Jesus. Knowing a few new moms myself, I'm sure that the last thing a woman needs who has just given birth is gold, frankincense, or myrrh, yet they are part of a larger theological picture that Matthew is trying to communicate. (I'm sure the new moms would take the gold, however!)

What do the actions of the Magi say to us today? I think their actions are relevant to us today on many levels. I think they can speak to us today concerning worship, silence, and gifts.

The wise men were focused. They knew why and to whom they had come. Their appropriate response was worship. There was no doubt for these visitors and no hesitation in worshiping in the presence of Mary and St. Joseph. There was no hesitation in giving their gifts freely to Jesus.

What is our attitude in worship? It may become methodical and routine if we forget for whom we are there.

As Catholics, even our body language of kneeling and standing speaks the language of worship, but if our hearts are far away then this will become an empty gesture. The visitors were there to offer worship and to give their gifts. This is contrary to people who go to church in hopes of receiving something or believe that they should be "entertained" at Mass. The Magi exhibited an attitude of gratitude.

Catholics kneel at the presence of Christ in the Eucharist, and rightfully so, but how do we respond to the presence of Christ when He's disguised in the poor, the marginalized, and the person right next to us at the checkout counter? Do we really recognize Jesus in the body of Christ, his Church? I dread to think of how reverent I am during Eucharistic adoration and how irreverent I am at times toward those around me who are also the presence of Christ.

This is not consistent with the gospel of Jesus. We can't be reverential toward Jesus in church and ignore those who are outside the church. Maybe it's my irreverence and my taking of these people for granted that contributes to their doubts about Christians and Christ. The Magi recognized Jesus for who He was, and we need to ask God for the same grace to recognize Him in our brothers and sisters.

Silence is a gift, too, that the Magi displayed and that worship can give us. Mary and St. Joseph are not recorded as saying a word when the gifts were presented, although I'm sure they were moved at the love, affection, and worship shown their son. Do we take advantage of those silent times in our lives?

Whether at Mass or in the car, silence can be a profound way for us to respond to God. Consider the fact that approximately 85 percent of the Bible takes place in the desert! No wonder God speaks in the silence of the heart to us today. If we don't have those silent times, we may never hear Him.

The Magi offered some strange gifts, humanly speaking. What is your gift? What do you bring to the manger? Unquestionably you and I have been blessed with many gifts. Do we categorize our gifts into spiritual gifts and natural gifts and somehow feel that the natural gifts are not as important as the spiritual? Any gift that you have can be brought to Jesus; after all, it is God who gave you those desires, gifts, and abilities.

A better question might be about our attitude toward our gifts. Do we freely offer them to Jesus and to others? Do we share our gifts with the realization that what we offer to others we really offer to Christ? Our knowledge of music, sports, finances, cooking, or whatever it may be is a gift and can be shared in the spirit of the Magi.

I always wonder at the gifts Jesus possessed, especially His miraculous powers. I'm amazed that He who fed the five thousand who were hungry would not use His own power to feed Himself while He was hungry in the desert. It makes me wonder about my own gifts and why God gave them to me. I'm certain that the lesson is that we are to use our gifts in the service of others.

Matthew, as well as songwriters and artists, have immortalized these Magi down through the ages. Let us remember that without a word they reverently and humbly presented their gifts before Christ. Let us consider asking God how can we best use our gifts.

The gift that Jesus left the Church was His Holy Spirit, who is our Advocate, the Spirit of truth who guides us. Pray that you and I may be attentive to the Spirit's leading and promptings, so that we, like the Magi, will freely give our gifts to Jesus.

SEVENTEEN

St. Joseph's Obedience

Matthew 1:24; 2:14, 21; Luke 2:48

When Joseph awoke, he did as the angel of the Lord had commanded him and took his wife into his home.... Joseph rose and took the child and his mother by night and departed for Egypt.... He rose, took the child and his mother, and went to the land of Israel.

When [Jesus'] parents saw him, they were astonished, and his mother said to him, "Son, why have you done this to us? Your father and I have been looking for you with great anxiety."

Without a doubt, he was more than a carpenter. Eighteen times St. Joseph is mentioned by name in the Gospels, and not once does he speak. Shrouded in anonymity from the beginning, his lack of words only adds to his mystery. He is as silent as all the statues, paintings, and stained glass with which the Church honors him.

Nevertheless, this mystery becomes unveiled to us as we examine his actions and where he shows up, especially in the early life of Jesus. His few mentions only accentuate his disposition as a man of faith who demonstrated protective love and provided stability for his family.

Early on in the Gospel story we are introduced to Joseph. He is betrothed to Mary and called "righteous."

*****

"Joseph, you must take a break, the heat is so oppressive!" said Nalla, Joseph's cousin and neighbor, who entered Joseph's workplace uninvited, as usual.

Joseph wiped the sweat from his brow with his arm, looked at Nalla, nodded and smiled, but continued on with his work. With a chisel in his left hand and a hammer in his right, he molded and crafted a long piece of ordinary olive wood into an object of beauty.

"Getting ready for your wedding, I see," Nalla continued, to some extent annoying Joseph and oblivious to his own intrusion. "Mary will very much enjoy all the preparation you've done. I bet she hasn't a clue about all the work you've put into this day."

Before Joseph could answer, Nalla turned and excused himself, mumbling something about an old donkey that was tethered out back, and then laughing to himself.

Unfortunately for Joseph, his wedding plans were not taking the expected route, for Mary was with child. The news had been quite a shock to Joseph; hundreds of thoughts and feelings bombarded his mind.

My parents and family, Joseph thought to himself as he contemplated his next move. *Mary's parents and family,* he mused, *we were getting along so nicely, and now this. What hurts me most is that I do love her, I do love her.*

Unwilling to expose Mary to shame, he decided to divorce her quietly.

Fatigued from the burden of such a sudden and traumatic crisis, Joseph lay down and tried to sleep. His physical labor was only a way of distracting himself from the recent, unsettling developments. Sleep, however, did not come easy, and he found himself tossing and turning in his bed, this recent news and his thoughts of Mary running through his head time and again. Finally, exhausted and hungry, he found sleep.

Then came a miracle as he slept. An angel of the Lord appeared to St. Joseph in a dream, addressed him by name, and revealed the startling news that Mary's child had been conceived through the Holy Spirit and that he should not be afraid to take her into his home.

No words of protest escaped his lips, no hesitation. Only obedience and trust. He did as the angel commanded.

*****

No wonder Joseph has been so highly honored by Christians throughout the ages.

During the period between Mary's revelation and Joseph's dream, what was Mary's state of mind? We are not told what she thought in Matthew's Gospel, but is there a chance that Joseph's obedience gave Mary comfort? Did Joseph's obedience during this time of crisis give Mary peace as God placed this man in her life?

I'd like to think so. I'd like to believe that when Joseph invited Mary over and showed her the room he had prepared for them and the living space for the soon-to-be-newborn that she thanked God for bringing this man into her life.

Shortly afterward we are told of another crisis, and again Joseph was present and obedient. This time, Jesus, the newborn, had His very existence threatened. It would not be the last time that people would seek His life.

Life for the newborn child's parents was no different in many aspects from that of present-day parents. Sleepless nights, changing diapers, waking up in the middle of the night to feed or comfort the crying infant were all part of this routine. But one night would be different.

Joseph had another dream. Again the angel of the Lord spoke to him, and told him to take the child and His mother to Egypt and to stay there. Joseph rose, took the child and Mary, and went. Out of obedience to God and protective love for Mary and Jesus, Joseph did the miraculous: He left.

Have you ever imagined what that might have been like for Joseph, to leave his familiar surroundings and travel to a foreign land at a moment's notice? Did he take the tools with which he made a living? Did he know the route? Did he speak Egyptian? Did he make arrangements for lodging? Was his extended family aware of his whereabouts? Did he wonder whether his baby and wife would survive the treacherous journey?

All of these questions remain unanswered. For Joseph, obedient and faithful, if God said "Go," he went. No counselors, no discernment process, just simple faith and obedience. Perhaps the faith of Abraham, who was also asked to go to a foreign land—and the precedent that God had asked him to do something once before in a dream and it had worked out for the best—gave him courage.

After Herod had died, this same sequence occurred in reverse; this time Joseph was to return to the land of Israel. It doesn't come as any surprise that he went. Obedient to God's timing, Joseph kept quiet and was obedient.

The last time in the Gospel of Luke that we read about Joseph is the occasion of another crisis. The holy family was going up to Jerusalem for their annual Passover celebration.

The way people traveled in the Middle East in the time of Joseph is important to understand, because it plays an essential part in this narrative. When traveling over long distances through rugged and dangerous terrain, there would be a men's group in the lead, followed by a women's and children's group, and picking up the rear would be another group of men. Thus, you would have protection both in front and from behind.

Since this was a Passover celebration, it is easy to imagine the whole village of Nazareth traveling together in a group, singing and telling stories as they approached the Holy City. Joseph would have been in one of the men's groups, with Mary and Jesus in the middle with the other women and children. It is with this understanding that we can see how Mary and Joseph each could have easily assumed that Jesus was with the other. After all, at twelve, Jesus was on his way to becoming a man, and it would have been quite easy for him to "move up" into the men's group.

We are told that after a day's journey, Mary and Joseph stopped, and after "comparing notes," discovered that Jesus was not with them. Mary and Joseph began their frantic search for their son among relatives and acquaintances. Only parents can truly relate to the panic that must have set in.

After three days, they found Him in Jerusalem in the temple, and it was Mary, with Joseph at her side, who spoke. Neither Mary nor Joseph understood Jesus' response, but it was Mary, we are told, who treasured all these things in her heart.

I've often wondered what Joseph thought. Did he, too, treasure these things? I'm not sure about "treasured," but remembered, most certainly.

What are we to make of the silent witness of Joseph for our lives today? Words can be important and powerful indeed, but often a strong example communicates more than any words can.

As I reflect on the silence of St. Joseph, I am struck by his place of honor in the Church. Certainly there are saints who wrote more, preached more effectively, attracted more converts. There are saints whom we know a great deal more about than he. Yet, when we think of Jesus, the holy family, Mary, there he is, often in the background, placed as a guardian of Jesus and a protector of Mary. What is it about him that has attracted such devotion by Christians throughout the years, and how can we imitate his virtues in our daily lives?

First of all, I am impressed by his attentiveness to God. He heard the voice of God and acted upon it. It was a voice that spoke to the very depth of his being, otherwise he wouldn't have taken action.

How can we put ourselves in a position to listen to God's voice in our lives? One way that God speaks is through the Scriptures. I find it helpful to read the Scriptures and let the words speak to me.

I don't have to read a whole chapter—maybe only a parable or a few verses. I find that if I ask God very specifically to speak to me through a passage, verse, or word before I read, then it puts me in a receptive position and opens me up to being more attentive. Often one word or short phrase will "pop out" at me and I'll reflect on it, mull it over throughout the day, and have it dwell in me.

Another way of being attentive to God's voice is making time to be still. It is a real gift to find a place with no distractions or interference and to just put yourself in God's presence for a period of time. I need to get out of the house and find a park or a church for me to effectively do this. I find myself too distracted at home or at work.

I also find it necessary to make a retreat and get away from the normal hustle and bustle of my routine at least once a year in order for me to put life in perspective and ask God for the grace to hear Him when He speaks.

Joseph was a man who displayed protective love during times of crisis. When things are going smoothly and life is going my way, it can be easy to be faithful and obedient to God, but when a crisis occurs I find that it reveals the quality and depth of my faith. Sometimes I come through with flying colors; at other times I am found lacking.

This lack of faith on my part causes me to reflect on where my faith ultimately lies, and it always leads me back to God.

When a crisis occurs in my life, I find solidarity with St. Joseph. In crises words are often inadequate to express the degree of confusion, suffering, or shock that we may be experiencing. St. Joseph faced these crises in his life and he quietly trusted.

Situations that might cause us to question God's will really don't need to cause us such doubt when we have approached the level of faith and trust of the saints. Saints are those men and women after whom we can model ourselves, because they "understood" God and lived out their lives in faith in an exemplary fashion.

By his silence St. Joseph communicated a rock-solid faith that trusted in God's will for him and his family. This type of faith didn't need to be expressed with words. In the same way that a child knows that his or her mother and father can be trusted, so, too, did Joseph model this faith in our heavenly Father for us.

Finally, I think of Joseph as the father of a teenager. The teenage years are years of growth and transition. While this can be an awkward time for the teenager, parents also have to deal with the changes that occur. This transition is not necessarily wrong or sinful, but it can be difficult. The body changes, relationships change, self-knowledge grows, and a desire for autonomy increases.

Jesus was growing in age and wisdom, and Mary and Joseph had to parent Him through these changes. We know that at least this one time Jesus caused them great anxiety. It must have been just as difficult for them to allow Jesus His freedom and departure from them as it is for parents today.

It would seem that Joseph and Mary did a pretty good job. The episode in the temple was not filled with screaming and curfews, although a curfew may have been discussed later. We are told only that they expressed their anxiety to Him and asked Him a question. Love lay behind both of these responses, and we hear of no other episodes like this.

Certainly Scripture scholars could argue that I'm reading too much into these incidents and that the Evangelists had their own reasons for telling us these stories, which may be more theologically based than based in reality. I do, however, think it's interesting to take the information that is given and ask what can it teach us, how we can apply it to our lives.

I wonder if many parents can relate to the anxiety of Mary and Joseph during the three days that their son was missing. Any parent who has a son or daughter who has just received his or her driver's license can answer that question, even if the time the child is missing is only three hours.

In the end, St. Joseph stood silently but not without witness. He had an obedient faith in God and a protective love for his family in times of crisis. Without a doubt, he was more than a carpenter.

EIGHTEEN

Ten Cleansed Lepers, Nine Were Silent

Luke 17:17-19

Jesus said in reply, "Ten were cleansed, were they not? Where are the other nine? Has none but this foreigner returned to give thanks to God?" Then he said to him, "Stand up and go; your faith has saved you."

Imagine being separated from everyone you care about, your friends, neighbors, and family. Envision those who are closest to you turning and running away as you draw near. You are not welcomed at your place of worship, at the marketplace, inside your own house, or even inside the city walls. Those whom you once turned away from in disgust have now become your community, your family.

The story of the ten cleansed lepers focuses our attention on the one man who returned to give thanks. This man, identified as a leper and a Samaritan, first approached Jesus in petition and then returned to give thanks to Jesus for the miracle cleansing that would allow him to return to the communion he had enjoyed with his family and community. We hold this man, a despised Samaritan no less, as an example of what a disciple is to do—namely, return to God to give thanks for His goodness.

But what about the other nine? What were they thinking, and what does their silence reveal?

Only Luke records for us this story highlighting the mercy and healing power of God through Jesus and the return of a cleansed leper to offer thanks to Jesus, the source of his healing. I often wonder about the other nine lepers who were cleansed. What was their story, and what can we learn from their apparent silence and failure to return to give thanks to Jesus?

*****

Raham woke up early, which was not unusual for him, because he still had difficulty getting accustomed to sleeping out of doors in the cool night air. The warmth of his wife lying next to him and the security that the walls of his house had once provided was a distant memory. He looked over at the assortment of men lying in close proximity and still couldn't believe that he was one of them, a leper.

During the past year, these men, whom he had once despised and avoided, had become his adopted family of sorts. Once they had been just "unclean" and "lepers," nameless men to be pitied. Now they were Jacob, Zedekiah, Saul, Haman, and the others, who all had stories similar to his, stories that were as tragic as his and as disheartening.

Of all the things that leprosy had taken away, his family, his job, and his dreams, what Raham missed the most was his dignity. His dignity had died the day the priest had identified the mark on his scalp as leprosy and pronounced him "unclean."

Raham had always thought of himself as part of a community. He had taken some pride in his appearance and the way he conducted himself wherever he went. All that had changed at the priest's pronouncement. Raham had liked who he was and had been comfortable with his body, but soon it became his enemy.

No longer could he embrace his wife and children, no longer could he enter the synagogue, and no longer could he work at his craft, which had been handed down to him from his father and his father's father before that. Life as he knew it had ended. He was now more concerned with survival than with living a meaningful life.

The news had not been received well by his family and friends, whom he had thought would be there to comfort him as they had in times past when tragedy struck. This development was different; this was leprosy. He understood that his ostracism was necessary because leprosy was a contagious disease, but he had never realized how much it demoralized a person until he himself had become a victim.

As Raham roused himself off his mat to begin another day of begging and trying to survive, he prayed. Zedekiah overheard his last line: "With my whole being I sing endless praise to you. O Lord, my God, forever will I give you thanks" (Ps 30:13).

"You haven't given up hope, have you?" questioned Zedekiah, startling Raham. Raham was caught off guard, having thought that he was the only one awake. "Not yet," he sheepishly replied. "Go back to bed, it's still early."

He dared not speak of the hope and faith that he possessed because of the mocking from his "friends," yet his faith in a merciful God was the only thing that kept him going day after day. The daily praying of the Psalms gave him a steady routine in which he was nourished spiritually, and focused him on the Lord.

Raham was a little embarrassed by being overheard in prayer. His faith in the Lord was a personal one. The stigma of leprosy and its association with sin troubled him as he tried to make sense of his condition. He had heard from the teachers of the Law that either he or his parents must have sinned in order for this misfortune to have befallen him. He struggled to make sense of it all and was torn between despair and hope.

Soon afterward, the rest of the leper community was up and about, making their plans for the day, which focused on one thing: food.

Jacob, the oldest of the lepers, held court as he usually did, giving instructions and staking out his own territory near the city gate.

"Haman, you go down the road a piece and call out to the travelers from the side of the road as they leave the city. Saul, you go with him and don't fall asleep, we need this to be a team effort."

Jacob knew exactly where the men needed to be so as to collect the most money and the best scraps of food from the people traveling to and from the city.

"Raham," Jacob shouted, "you go up the road with Zedekiah and gesture to the people passing by. Keep your words few, just look hungry."

Just look hungry, Raham thought. *That won't be too difficult to do.*

"Come on, Zedekiah," beckoned Raham sarcastically, "we have to go and *look hungry*."

As they were leaving, Jacob warned them, "Remember, do not get anywhere near the people, they will only run from you if you get too close." Raham said rhetorically, "Do we really need to be reminded of that?" Off they went up the road together, two men in the same circumstance hoping to get some money for food or food itself.

It didn't take long before a group of men came down the road. "Raham, look hungry, here come some people," said Zedekiah with a sarcastic grin, but the men just walked by and ignored the two beggars. There wasn't much either of them could say, for they, too, had walked by countless beggars in their day when they were "healthy."

"Here come some more," motioned Raham to a despondent Zedekiah. "Don't worry, my friend, I think these people will be generous."

"Food, food?" said Raham from a distance, "if you could spare anything we will forever be in your debt. Alms for some poor lepers? Alms?"

"I have no food on me, nor money," shouted a man in reply to their request, "but I'll tell you this, Jesus of Nazareth is soon coming this way. He's headed toward Jerusalem. It's been reported that the power of the Almighty works through Him. Maybe He can give you something."

Zedekiah thought aloud, "Jesus, that's not the first time I have heard His name. Maybe He's the answer to your prayer this morning?"

"Let's go tell the others," said Raham, and without hesitation they returned to Jacob, who was near the city gate. With elation they explained the news that they had heard regarding Jesus.

"Jesus of Nazareth?" asked Jacob, wanting to make sure which Jesus they had heard was coming. Jacob put his hand to his chin and said, "Are you sure He's coming this way?" "That's what we were told," Raham and Zedekiah said together. "Then we must gather the others quickly."

Jacob, being the oldest, was usually impervious to the news of "healers" and "miracle cures," for he had been escorted along that road before, only to be cheated out of his money. Yet he had heard of this Jesus of Nazareth and decided that He was worth a look for himself. After all, what did he have to lose?

With the determination of an army general, Jacob quickly gave orders to round up the others and to gather a half mile up the road so as to meet Jesus before He reached town. Raham and Zedekiah did as they were told and proceeded to round up the others.

Within the hour, Jesus came down the road with a group of men and women following close behind. It was difficult to pick out which one was Jesus, because they couldn't get too close.

"Jesus, Master! Have pity on us," they shouted as one, making sure that they were a respectful distance from Him.

Jesus stopped, approached them, and said, "Go show yourselves to the priests." It was a short, simple encounter. Raham somehow expected a little more, but he didn't know exactly what. "Show yourselves to the priests?" He repeated aloud the words of Jesus and was somewhat taken aback.

In faith they did as Jesus had said, following the directions for a person cleansed from leprosy as prescribed in the Book of Leviticus.

While they were on their way, one of them, a Samaritan, noticed that he was cleansed and decided to go back to Jesus to offer Him thanks and praise. The other nine noticed that they too were cleansed. The white blotches that had covered their bodies were gone.

In excitement and wonder the nine continued on their way, considering aloud what they would do next. The possibilities were endless. Things of which they had previously only dreamed could now become a reality.

Secure in the knowledge of his healing, the Samaritan retraced his steps and went back to Jesus. He approached, glorifying God with a loud voice, fell at Jesus' feet, and thanked Him. Never before had he been so close to God, physically and spiritually.

"Ten were cleansed, were they not? Where are the other nine?" Jesus asked rhetorically. "Has none but this foreigner returned to give thanks to God?" Jesus continued, "Stand up and go; your faith has saved you."

*****

Where was Raham? Where were the other nine altogether? God healed them also through their encounter with Jesus. Nevertheless, we are left to wonder why they never came back to thank Him. Jesus didn't condemn them or reverse the healing but rather commended the one who returned, a Samaritan.

I don't think the other nine cleansed lepers were "bad people"; they just didn't return to offer thanks to Jesus, the source of their healing. I don't say that lightly, because Jesus did ask where they were. He was expecting ten, I presume.

Could it have been that a few were so excited they ran home to embrace their wives and kids? Could you blame them? Did some do as Jesus said and go to the priests to be examined? Did one of them go to Jerusalem to offer sacrifice in the temple? Did Raham break down and weep with joy, knowing that he was restored to his former way of life and all of his former relationships? We'll never know for sure.

This miracle does challenge my "attitude of gratitude," or lack of it at times. I would like to think that I give God His rightful thanks and praise for who He is and for all that He's done in my life, but I'm afraid that more often than not I identify with the nine lepers, and that bothers me.

Jesus did not run after the nine, forcing "praise and thanks," but He did wonder where they were. Jesus is not trying to make us feel guilty over our lack of appreciation, but I think He desires to join with us in our celebration and joy. I'm convinced that He wants to be involved in our lives and, as the psalmist says, to give us the desires of our heart (see Ps 37:4).

All the lepers called out to Jesus in faith and hope. They even addressed Him with honor by calling Him "Master." Jesus immediately responded by telling them to show themselves to the priests, and they followed His direction.

Yet why did only this one man come back? Certainly all ten lepers were made whole and remained whole. Jesus did not give the nine a new case of leprosy; He did not punish them for failing to return.

Love is not like that. Love freely gives and builds up; it seeks the good of the other even when the other may not show thanks or appreciation. Love also does not keep a record of wrongs but rejoices in the truth, as we are reminded by the words of St. Paul (see 1 Cor 13:6).

We are reminded at the cross that Jesus died for and forgave even those who crucified Him. The leper came back because that's what love does, that's what a disciple of Jesus does—returns to give thanks.

I must ask myself after reading this story where and when I need to return to give thanks to God and to others. For me it begins with the Eucharist, which literally means "thanksgiving." The Mass is the apex and pinnacle of worship and thanksgiving. In the Mass, as a community and as individuals we give thanks to Jesus, we proclaim through word and sacrament His goodness and our thanks.

After we return home from our gathering at the Eucharistic table, the family table is another good place to start to say thanks.

Our thankfulness to God can be expressed in many wonderful ways. Prayer and song can be a beautiful way to convey gratitude. Speaking to God from our hearts can be a very expressive and spontaneous way of responding to God. Reciting formal prayers from a book or prayer card can often articulate what we feel inside but can't quite verbalize on our own. Including Jesus in all aspects of our lives is a way of saying thanks, for in doing that we recognize Him as the source of all goodness.

We can take action and serve others in the name of God as a way of response: "I'm giving back to God because He has done great things for me." Organizing friends and people in our parishes and communities also reflects the spirit of appreciation. However, before this can take place, we need to return to Jesus.

Humbly, like the Samaritan who prostrated himself before Jesus, we need to bring ourselves to His feet, to His mercy. Without first bringing ourselves to Jesus, it's easy to forget why we're performing the act of charity, or even worse, to inflate our own egos and give praise to ourselves rather than to God.

Whatever we do, we should keep in mind the Samaritan who in freedom and love returned to God. Our attitude should be one of appreciation and gratefulness and never fear or guilt. The thought that God might "get me" for not being grateful is not a Christian idea. We give thanks always because of love; God is good and worthy of our thanks and praise, no matter what the circumstances in our lives may be.

Jesus tells the man that his faith has saved him. The Samaritan isn't recorded as saying a word; his thanks was evident in his position before Jesus. Meanwhile, the other nine are never heard from again in Scripture, and their witness is a poor one.

While the nine cured lepers may have given thanks in time, I wonder about the failed opportunity to go right to the source of their healing—namely, Jesus. We, too, can go to the source, because Jesus is alive and well today; it's never too late to give thanks.

Let us follow the example of the Samaritan. We must return often to God to thank Him for our lives and for all that God is and all that He continues to do in our lives and in the world as we walk with Him.

NINETEEN

The Baptism of Jesus

Matthew 3:16-17

After Jesus was baptized, he came up from the water and behold, the heavens were opened [for him], and he saw the Spirit of God descending like a dove [and] coming upon him. And a voice came from the heavens, saying, "This is my beloved Son, with whom I am well pleased."

This is my beloved Son, with whom I am well pleased." Wow! Who wouldn't love to hear those words resounding from heaven? What a great affirmation of the Father's love for Jesus.

If you read what Jesus has accomplished up to this point in regard to His public ministry, these words are even more remarkable. A careful reading of the first three chapters of Matthew reveals that Jesus has done nothing of any significance in terms of ministry. He hasn't preached a sermon, He hasn't told any parables, and He hasn't performed any miracles.

These are all things that we associate with Jesus and His public ministry, and up to this point they are missing. Yet the words of God are crystal clear: *"This is my beloved Son, with whom I am well pleased."*

What those words must have done for Jesus as He began His ministry are the same things that those words can do for you and me—namely, assure us of the Father's love, regardless of what we do.

Before Jesus started His ministry He had the assurance of the Father's love. God was and is well pleased with Him for who Jesus is and not for any particular thing that He did. How often do we hear those words in our lives?

"You are beloved and I am well pleased with you for who you are, not for what you may do or accomplish or achieve." We may hear accolades after twenty-five years of service at work, after an athletic achievement, or maybe during school when we have accomplished something of significance. But to hear such praise out of the blue is something else.

Immediately after Jesus' baptism the Spirit led Him into the desert and Satan tempted Him and attacked Him. With what did Satan attack and tempt Jesus? It wasn't sin, because for Jesus sin would not have been attractive or tempting. Satan attacked Jesus' identity, who He was in relation to the Father.

The first word out of Satan's mouth was "if": "*If* you are the Son of God." What a fool Satan was! "*If* you are the Son of God." Jesus had just heard the words from heaven assuring Him, *"Yes, you are my beloved Son."* But that didn't stop Satan from trying to deceive Jesus.

Jesus responded to these attacks with the sword of the Spirit, the Word of God, not bad advice for us when we are attacked. The Word of God assured Jesus of his *Sonship.* Were those words lost on Jesus? I think not.

Ask yourself how you have responded to an affirmation from another person. Whether the person affirming us is a parent, an office worker, a teacher, or a spouse, he or she usually does impact us in a positive way. The power of those words can even sustain us through difficult times. We may not look any different, but the change that takes place with affirmation is an internal one.

In this passage God affirmed the love He had for Jesus and Jesus' relationship to God as Son. However, a question remained: Who are you, and where do you get your identity?

In silence, Jesus heard the words of the Father, "This is my beloved Son, with whom I am well pleased," and He didn't immediately respond. No response to the voice is recorded by the Gospel writer, but as we examine the life of Jesus and especially the temptation, it seems clear that Jesus must have reflected on these words and drawn power from them.

Do we fall for the trap of Satan, who tries to assault our relationship with God and ultimately our identity? Do we believe that we are beloved for what we do instead of who we are in Christ? What is it about our understanding of God and our baptism that we would ever call into question God's love for us and our identity as sons and daughters of God? Is it because it seems too good to be true? Is it because we have been conditioned to believe that we will be accepted and loved *only* if we behave well and accomplish great things?

Unfortunately, the notion that God's love is too good to be true is not new. In the parable of the Great Banquet (see Lk 14), the servant was told to go into the highways and hedgerows and *compel* the people to come to the feast. They had to be compelled to enter the house because the invitation was too unbelievable. Such is God's love for His children.

If we were baptized as infants we were claimed for God, declared sons and daughters of God before we even knew what was going on. God's love and the Christian community's love were extended to us even before we could respond, before we had *accomplished* anything. If we were baptized as adults we were more conscious of what we were doing and saying, but the message is the same: We are God's beloved.

What does unconditional love do for a person? Do I adopt the attitude that "I don't have to do anything because I'm so loved, regardless of what I do?" Hopefully not, because those who do know God's love are also compelled to reach out to others in love and friendship, in order to share that love.

Unconditional love frees us from the fear of failure. It frees us from the pressure of trying to earn God's love. We can take risks because we know who we are: *beloved of the Father.* That knowledge of God's personal and abiding love for us is something that Jesus knew in the deepest part of His humanity. When He faced Satan He could respond with the same Word of God that assured Him of who He was.

Satan attacked Jesus with the words "If you are the Son of God" once again, at the end of His ministry, when Jesus was on the cross. Jesus did not come down but relied on God, whose will He was fulfilling.

Assurance and faith of God's love for us spills over into quiet confidence, the same quiet confidence that Jesus possessed. He came up out of the water silent but not unchanged. It was this certainty, dependence, belief, and hope that allowed Him to be led into the desert and come out the victor. It allowed Him to enter into towns and villages that were hostile to Him and proclaim God's love.

As you and I go about our daily lives, we will have our identity attacked. We will have our faith in a God who loves us as we are, with our sin and imperfections, ridiculed. We will be tempted to base our relationship with God on what we do rather than on who we are.

Society will give us the message that money and status are what makes us important and worthwhile. The business world will tell us that we need to be productive in order to be someone. Our institutions of learning may send the message that only if we achieve a certain degree of academic success are we important. The world of fashion insists that if we don't have the current "look" or we are not youthful and thin, then we are not valuable.

The idea of not being *beloved* in the eyes of God can even creep into ministry. We may judge our "success" by the standards of how many people are involved or how big our ministry is instead of our faithfulness to His call.

When those times come, let us remember Jesus as He came out of the waters, as well as our own baptism, so that in silence we can hear a God who says to our hearts, "You are my beloved, and I am well pleased with you!"

TWENTY

The Good, Silent Samaritan

Luke 10:36-37

*"Which of these three, in your opinion, was neighbor to the robbers'
victim?" He answered, "The one who treated him with mercy." Jesus
said to him, "Go and do likewise."*

Jerusalem sits 2,700 feet above sea level on top of Mount Zion.
Jericho, seventeen miles to the east, lies eight hundred feet below sea
level. Of all the roads in the Middle East, the one road that you don't
want to travel alone is the one from Jerusalem to Jericho. The thirty-
five-hundred-foot descent on this road winds through some of the
world's roughest terrain and in ancient times was treacherous because
of the brigands, outlaws, and robbers who made it their home.

The rugged, dangerous, and deep crevasses wind through valleys,
making travel all the more risky. It is also problematic because the far-
ther you travel down the road, the more unbearable the heat becomes
as it beats down upon you as you head toward one of the lowest places
on the face of the earth. You will find no shade, no resting spots, no
inns in which to find comfort before you reach the Jewish town of
Jericho.

It is on this road that Jesus tells of a man, a Samaritan, whose com-
passionate actions define what it is to be a neighbor and how a person
should love.

*****

"You'll be going home in a few days," said Laban to Saul the priest. "I envy you."

"Yes, two days from now I head home to my wife, children, and farm. I can't wait to get back. I can almost hear my children running and playing in the street, and my wife is an excellent cook." Saul smiled to himself as the bright sun reflected off his face.

"You are valuable here, too, Saul, and the people like you."

Saul nodded, "I am fortunate to have such good people around me, and I take my priestly duties seriously. Being a priest of the Lord carries with it great responsibilities, but still I miss my family. Being a priest makes me no less human."

Their priestly duties had brought Laban and Saul together; each had responsibilities in the temple every year for a two-week period.

The days passed quickly, and Saul bid farewell to Laban. He also took leave of the others who stayed behind and made Jerusalem their home.

"Be careful, Saul," pleaded Laban. "We both know that the way you are going home is the fastest but also the most dangerous. Have you considered waiting a while so you can join a group of men who are also going that way?"

"I'll take my chances," replied Saul. "Pray that the Lord will watch over me."

With that confidence Saul left the temple area and soon disappeared into the crowded streets. He headed east toward the Wadi ar Rawabi and the road that would soon bring him home. He followed it with hopes of seeing his family later that night; if he made good time he would make it home before midnight.

Saul traveled uneventfully all morning by himself, often looking over his shoulder so as not to be surprised or overtaken by robbers. He could have waited until later that day to travel with a caravan but he wanted to get home that same day. Jericho was home to over five thousand priests, and he was hopeful that he might find a traveling companion on the way.

A short time after three in the afternoon, while the sun was still high in the cloudless sky, Saul noticed an object a few hundred feet down the road, on the right shoulder. He put his right hand up to his forehead to shield his eyes from the sun. At first he thought it might be the carcass of an animal but as he drew nearer the reality of the situation became clearer.

What is that? Saul asked himself, watching his steps on the uneven ground. *It can't be a man, can it?* He looked to his left, to his right, and then behind himself. He slowly drew opposite the man, and that was all he knew, that it was, in fact, a man.

As Saul approached this beaten and forsaken man he looked for any clues as to his identity. *Clothes*, Saul thought, *where are his clothes? This could reveal if he was a Jew.* No clothes were to be found. If the man had given in to his robbers they would have most likely taken only his money, but apparently he had unsuccessfully put up a fight and they had beaten him and stripped him.

Saul looked at the beaten man from afar and wondered if the man would speak or utter a sound. Saul thought, *If he speaks Hebrew then I might be able to offer some aid, perhaps even his accent might give me a clue as to his origin.* However, no words escaped the parched lips of this beaten man. This strange scene found two men on the road to Jericho, one helpless and the other unwilling to help.

Saul took one last look and noticed dried blood on the face and arms of the destitute man, who lay there naked with no voice and now no hope. He deliberated momentarily and determined that his next move would be to walk around the man and head on toward Jericho.

It has been two long weeks since I last saw my family, Saul thought briefly, as he departed. *If I touch this man I will become ritually unclean, and I will have to go back up to Jerusalem for a seven-day purification ceremony involving water and the ashes of a red heifer, as prescribed in the Book of Leviticus. Seven days away from my family, seven days away from my land. I don't even know who he is, if he's a Jew or one of them.*

Satisfied with his rationale and reasoning, Saul headed home, leaving the nameless man behind.

Not too long afterward, a Levite came along the same road. He also immediately saw the problem of touching a man who was "unclean" and perhaps a foreigner, and he, too, passed by on the other side.

By chance, a Samaritan who was coming down the road saw the man and was moved with compassion. No words passed his lips, no concern for his own safety, only a heart moved with compassion for another human being who was in need. He didn't wonder who the man was or if he was a Jew or a Samaritan, or even a foreigner, for that matter; he just saw a man in need.

He approached the victim and offered assistance. The victim was foolish for traveling alone; nevertheless, the Samaritan did not hesitate in giving him aid. He poured oil and wine on the man's wounds, and, dropping to one knee, he turned the man over on his side to bandage his face and arms.

With care and considerable effort, the Samaritan bent at the knees as he moved his arms under the legs and back of the victim; he lifted him up and placed him atop his own animal. All the while, the man was still unresponsive and unconscious. The Samaritan's hands and clothes were soiled with the dirt and dried blood that were on the injured man.

Then the Samaritan had a decision to make: Should he bring him into Jericho? Jericho was a Jewish city with a large Jewish population. What would they think when they saw this despised enemy, this Samaritan, walk through the city to the inn, in plain view of everybody, with an injured man on his animal? Yet, what other choice did he have?

The Samaritan brought him to the only inn there was, the one in Jericho. The townspeople stared as he led his animal down the main street. The business in the crowded street stopped as people turned their heads to watch this perplexing scene. Slowly and resolutely, the Samaritan made his way to the inn, towing his animal behind him.

After checking in, the Samaritan stayed with the man overnight, making sure that his needs were attended to. Only then did he speak. His words were few, but, like his actions, showed that he had the best interest of the victim in mind. "Take care of him. If you spend more than what I have given you, I shall repay you on my way back."

*****

This wonderful parable of Jesus, which can be read in about thirty seconds, demonstrates what love is, as illustrated by the actions of the Samaritan. This parable continues to challenge people of all backgrounds and origins with the recognition and treatment of our neighbors.

Jesus tells this parable in response to a question, "Who is my neighbor?" The answer that the lawyer in the story gave, "The one who treated him with mercy," was in fact the correct answer, although the lawyer himself had a difficult time saying the word *Samaritan.*

The question we must grapple with is who we are really like—the priest, the Levite, or the Good Samaritan—and if it is the Samaritan, how that translates into our everyday life.

The details of the story challenge our response to those whom we pass along the way each and every day. The victim was traveling alone, a very foolish thing to do, and the fact that he fell among robbers is of no surprise, we almost expect it to happen; yet, the Samaritan didn't withhold his aid. This causes me to reflect upon the people in my life who by their own foolishness or recklessness are always getting into trouble. I know they are going down the "wrong road"; I've even warned them about it because it's easy to see where it will end—in disaster.

Is there a temptation on my part to withhold my aid or care toward them? Sometimes we may see the tragedy coming from "miles away," yet the person may go through with his or her plan and fall flat on his or her face. Is there a temptation to say, "I told you so," and to let the person wallow in misery for awhile? It is then that the actions of the Good Samaritan should come to mind.

How many times has God come to my assistance even though His Word had warned me I was in peril? How many times has God gently taken care of me in spite of my foolishness when I've fallen? If God acts this way toward us, can we act differently toward others?

The victim in the story had no identity; his lack of clothing and voice robbed him of that which is sometimes more important to us than it should be. Are there people from whom we withhold our love because they are not "one of us"?

Maybe they are not citizens of our country. Perhaps they worship at another church or in another denomination. Maybe we are intimidated because of their age, whether they are young or old.

What if they are believers in a religion different from our own, or what if they are atheists? I like to belong to groups of people who share my interests and hobbies, and many of my friends share the same religious beliefs as I do. But if I withhold help to other people based on those outward or interior criteria, then I am in serious danger of being at odds with Christ.

The priest did have a reason why he didn't offer help—namely, the sacrifice of his time and family that would be involved in the seven-day cleansing ritual. In light of the praise Jesus gave the lawyer for choosing the Samaritan, do we have a choice do to otherwise?

Love doesn't count the cost; it acts in spite of the cost. What may be the cost to you for stopping to help someone? Will it mean that you're late for a sports game or a meeting at the local diner? Will it mean that you can't go out with your friends because this person needs your help?

People usually need help at inconvenient times. Will you respond freely and lovingly or will you walk on by? As I write this, the answer I want to give is yes, but I wonder if that's what I witness through my actions.

Another detail that I find interesting is that the victim didn't cry out for help; the Samaritan noticed him and stopped. Are there people in your life and mine that aren't verbally crying out for help yet could use our help and a hand? These people are present among us. We need to ask God for the grace to see and hear as He does so that we don't miss these opportunities to witness to our belief that every person is valuable and created in the image of God.

The victim was unresponsive to the assistance given him, and we don't read of the victim saying thank you. Yet that does not stop the love shown to him. In this story the victim is physically unable to say thanks.

In our lives of ministry we will meet people who are also unable to say thanks. Maybe they just can't find the words, maybe they have forgotten, or possibly they, too, are physically unable to verbalize their gratefulness. Nevertheless, we have to focus on love, and love is more concerned with the welfare of the other than with the praise and recognition we may or may not receive for our actions.

The action of the Samaritan put him in danger of physical harm. Jesus used a Samaritan to highlight the supremacy of love that would have stood in contrast to the legalism of the priest in the story. The Samaritans and the Jews had a long-standing hatred for each other, which only highlighted the actions of Samaritan that Jesus used as the hero of the story while speaking to a Jewish audience.

This reality reminds me that there is a cost to following Christ, and at times discipleship may put us in harm's way. I do not suggest that we actively seek out dangerous situations, which may only call attention to ourselves, because this is the essence of pride. However, our rich tradition holds in honor those men and women who have sacrificed themselves and even been killed for giving witness. Perhaps more practical for us are those everyday situations that call us to die to ourselves. These "little deaths" witness to the sacrifice we are called to make if we follow Christ.

Archeologists have not discovered any evidence of inns or places of lodging along this dangerous road. That leads us to the conclusion that the Samaritan took the victim into Jericho, which was enemy territory due to the long history of distrust and hatred between Jews and Samaritans.

This Samaritan put his life on the line; he sacrificed not only his money but also his safety to care for this stranger. As we go through our day, there may be those occasions where we might be put to the test and have to risk our safety. For some of us this may mean venturing into new areas to do ministry; for others it may mean going out of our comfort zone to reach out in love across boundaries, whatever they may be.

In my own life, leaving my comfort zone has involved going to nursing homes, a veteran's hospital, and various migrant outreaches. These places are my Jerichos, places that I don't usually frequent and where I feel a little out of place, but they have enabled me to be touched by others who have so much to offer.

I am challenged by the actions of the Samaritan; there are still people in my life that I pass by because I don't want to get my hands dirty with their messy life problems. There are those for whom the cost of stopping appears fruitless and a waste of time. At those instances when I am cynical, I remember the compassion of the Samaritan and the compassion of Jesus, who stops daily to get involved in my messy life. I remember that no act of love escapes the eyes of God or is unimportant.

Our actions do reveal what is important in our lives, and the actions of Jesus and the Good Samaritan reveal a profound respect for the dignity of every human being. We may have good excuses and rationalize our behavior, but this only emphasizes that living the Christian life is not always easy. Sacrifice rarely is. It is, however, worth it.

Without words we live what we believe every day. The kindness we extend to others, the times we stop to check on a friend or to joke with a stranger at the diner, all these little gestures are our witness to living as Jesus lived. After all, it is Jesus who stops for you and me, even when we make the same mistake over and over again and get ourselves in all sorts of trouble.

He still bends down to pick us up when the world beats us up and we get knocked down, and in the end He will not take us to an inn but to the Father's house. This we can be sure of.

TWENTY-ONE

The Healing Touch: A Touching Response

Mark 1:29-31

On leaving the synagogue he entered the house of Simon and Andrew with James and John. Simon's mother-in-law lay sick with a fever. They immediately told him about her. He approached, grasped her hand, and helped her up. Then the fever left her and she waited on them.

Usually when a person thinks of the miraculous, great images come to mind. If we are familiar with the Hebrew Scriptures we may think of the parting of the Red Sea, the manna falling from heaven, the plagues that befell Egypt, or the pillar of fire that led the Israelites. In the New Testament when we think of the miraculous we tend to think of the Incarnation, Jesus walking on the water, the multiplication of the loaves and fish, the raising of Lazarus, and the Resurrection.

We usually don't think of this miracle, however—a small one: the healing of Simon's mother-in-law, as recorded by Matthew, Mark, and Luke. I'm not sure whose idea it was, but after leaving the synagogue somebody invited Jesus into the house. What a difference that invitation made!

*****

"Have you ever heard preaching like that?" exclaimed Navi as he and his companions left the synagogue.

"Never," said Alphaeus. "His teaching was astounding, yes, but then the rebuke of the unclean spirit! I have never witnessed anything like that in all my life. The Spirit of God is definitely moving in that man, Jesus!"

The synagogue service was over and the Jewish congregation at Capernaum ambled out of the synagogue, each amazed by what they had just heard and witnessed. The Sabbath was at hand, a day for God, family, and rest.

"Jesus, you would do me and my family great honor if you would eat with us today," said Simon eagerly, anxious to spend time with the man he and his companions had just left their nets to follow.

"It would be my honor, Simon. I have much to talk about with you and Andrew as well as the brothers James and John." Jesus grabbed Simon's shoulder, and with a smile they walked to his home.

Immediately the first disciples told Jesus that there was a sickness in the home. Simon's mother-in-law was sick with a fever. It was a common ailment, she was a common person, and yet this provoked an extraordinary response from Jesus.

Simon's mother-in-law lay in bed. A fever had taken hold of her. In time, no doubt, the fever would pass and she would be able to tend to the daily tasks of her household. Miserable and despondent for the moment, however, she lay in bed listening to the sound of people filling her house. Being a mother, she most likely wanted to prepare food for her guests and provide proper hospitality, but the fever held a grip on her and she could not get out of bed to serve.

Immediately upon hearing of the sickness, Jesus brushed aside the curtain that separated the room and entered. He looked at the woman, grasped her hand, and helped her up. The fever left her and she was healed. Silently, Jesus came back to his disciples.

Normally the mother-in-law might be heard saying, "Jesus, recline over here, Simon and Andrew, over there. Ah, James and John, you're here again! Jesus, these two are like my own sons, they're here so often." Yet, this time, after experiencing the touch of Jesus, she served in silence, overwhelmed by the touch of Christ.

*****

The unnamed woman, touched by Jesus, herself became a disciple and silently served them. How powerful was the touch of Jesus! Somebody cared, somebody reached out, even though it was just a common fever, and now she did the same. The impact of that healing reached far beyond the inner room where they ate. Immediately after the mother-in-law served them, when sundown arrived, we are informed that the people brought to Jesus all who were sick or possessed by demons, and we are told that Jesus cured many.

We are informed that they "gathered around the door." This woman opened up her home so others might receive the same healing touch that she had herself received.

We are not told whether Jesus or His companions initiated the invitation into the home that day in Capernaum, but what an impact having Jesus in the home made! Regardless of who initiated the invitation, Jesus was welcome and His presence made a tremendous difference. Simon's mother-in-law responded by silently serving. No words were needed in order to respond to the touch of Jesus. Then she opened her home to others in hospitality and love.

When I reflect on this miracle and the events that surround it, I ask myself if Jesus is a welcome guest in my home, my workplace. Certainly by sign and symbol Jesus can be present. A crucifix, a pious statue, or an icon can remind my friends and myself that Jesus is welcome here.

Perhaps He is invited and welcomed by a blessing before a meal, a family rosary, or a prayer before retiring to sleep. There are many ways in which our outward piety can be a witness to the presence of Christ.

Jesus is also invited in and present in a loving embrace, an act of patience, the sacrificial act of cleaning and cooking, and in countless other ways by our actions. He can be present in a lunch or dinner invitation or in an open invitation to "come to our house."

Unfortunately, there are times when I forget to invite Jesus into my home, due to absentmindedness, the hectic pace of life, or the thought that creeps into my mind once in a while that Jesus has bigger problems to handle than my little, "insignificant" troubles. At those times I call to mind this miracle and I'm reminded that nothing is "little" or "insignificant" in the eyes of Jesus. It's all important to Him, because I am important to Him. Jesus hears my prayer, He cares, and He has the ability and the desire to help.

When I go deeper in my reflection, I must ask myself if there are rooms in my house that are off-limits to Jesus. Certainly He is welcome in my family room and kitchen, but are there "closets" and "basements" that I would rather not have Jesus enter? After all, most of our lives, like our homes (or at least mine), have some clutter, areas that need some straightening out and junk that we need to get rid of.

It's important to remember that clutter never prevents Jesus from accepting our invitation to come into our lives. He loves to "clean house" and help us get our affairs in order. He won't, however, force Himself into a place where He's not welcome. He may knock, but we have to open the door to let Him in. I have to ask myself if all of my rooms and closets are welcoming and open to Jesus.

The disciples knew about the illness in the house and they simply told Jesus about it. What is my reaction when there is a problem? I need to take the lead of the disciples and tell Jesus about it. No matter how small, no problem is small in the eyes of God.

The first thing that drew me to this miracle was the silent action of Jesus. There have been times when I, too, have been present when somebody was sick and hurting and I have wished that I had the words to help, heal, or make things right. This miracle reminds me that often it's the silent touch, hug, and embrace that bring healing and relief.

Rarely do we remember what words people spoke to us in our time of need, but we do remember their presence. How often have our actions, be they a pat on the back, a smile, or a helping hand, raised somebody up? I'm sure that it is more often than we are aware of.

In those times when we notice that somebody is sad or "not himself" (or herself), and we go out of our way to show that person support or care, we are in a significant way continuing the mission of Jesus. That is what being a disciple of Christ is all about.

The disciples invited Jesus into their home, and that home was never again the same. When we allow Jesus into our homes, families, and workplaces, they, too, will not remain the same. His touch continues through you and me. Let us respond as the nameless mother-in-law did, in service. When those times occur when we don't have the words to lift others out of their suffering and heartache, let us respond with the touch of Christ that we ourselves have received from God. We have great power to bring the healing touch that Jesus brought so many years ago.

Imagine when you are no longer here and your story is being told. People will most likely not sit around recalling all the wonderful things you said, but rather the things that you did. We have a great capacity to be good, to do good, and to be a power for good.

TWENTY-TWO

The Man With the Restored Hand

Luke 6:10

Looking around at them all, he then said to him, "Stretch out your hand." He did so and his hand was restored.

We identify ourselves in many different ways, by our family name, in relationship to others, by our occupation, by our school, or even by some accomplishment. Imagine being identified by a physical deformity!

Not many people like to be at center stage or the focus of controversy, and in fact most of us do our best to keep a relatively low profile. In this miracle story, a nameless man with a withered hand who was at the synagogue was called by Jesus to take center stage, and his life was changed forever.

*****

A week after the historic visit of Jesus to the synagogue, you travel to the town where the man with the withered hand lives to ask him and those who witnessed the miracle their recollections of what happened and to see for yourself if this truly transpired in the way that you've been hearing.

Drawing near the town, you first notice the thick, rich scent of grain that is in the air, which is a pleasant reprieve from the often-foul smell of fish that permeates the towns along the coast. Spring is at hand, and while this means warmer weather, long hours of work lie ahead in the days to come. The upcoming Sabbath will provide the rest and refreshment for the soul that is not only sought after but also the Jewish Law.

You close your eyes and imagine the habitual routine of the towns-people as they enter the synagogue: friends slinging their arms around each other and talking while gradually the men and women take their separate places on the benches within. Inside the synagogue the dusty streets are a memory as the Torah is taken out and is revered with honor as the leader begins to read the appointed portion.

"Our minds were focused on the reading," recalls Josiah as he reminisces about that day, "but there was a strange tension in the air that couldn't be denied. Jesus was present, and all of us were curious as to what He would do."

Josiah continues, shading his eyes from the brutal midday sun, "We had all heard of the signs that Jesus had supposedly performed in other synagogues, and rumors spread that He had broken the Law by picking grain on the Sabbath. We were curious to see if He would say or do anything controversial or miraculous here. We had not yet made up our minds about Him."

Rachael speaks up and says, "This Jesus character and His disheveled disciples didn't much impress me or the crowd by their looks when they first approached, to be quite honest. Then He stood up and began to teach. That's when we all took notice. There was no denying that the Spirit of the Lord was with Him."

She calls this to mind as she is sitting in the entrance of her tent while mending her husband's garment. She is a frail woman with strong, bony hands, and she continues speaking without losing the rhythm of her stitching.

"Immediately you could tell that this man was special. His voice resonated with authority and He taught as one who not only knew about God but also knew Him personally. That's my opinion, anyway," and she looks up as if to add something, but no words come.

Asa, who has overheard the conversation, speaks up and adds, "The hair on the back of my neck stood up when He talked about false piety and hypocrisy, all the time gazing directly at the scribes and Pharisees. We could all sense their obvious disgust with Jesus but He didn't change his tone or message. He was firm and spoke with conviction. The anger and dirty looks of the Pharisees only added to their guilt. They had come to our synagogue quite unexpectedly and they seemed to stir and become restless and agitated as Jesus spoke. I was sitting right next to one of them; I remember how good this one Pharisee smelled and how angry he became."

As Asa finishes speaking, you turn to explore the town and interview more people about their recollection of the events. Just as you turn to leave, however, a voice speaks aloud ...

"Then He turned to me."

It is him, the man with the withered hand.

"Those eyes stared right at me as Jesus said, 'Come up and stand before us.'"

Could it really be him? The man whom Jesus spoke to and healed just a short week ago? He offers you a seat and quietly you soak up his story like a bone-dry sponge in a monsoon. The restored man recalls some of his life and the life-changing events of the last Sabbath.

"For all of my life up to that point I had to struggle with doing even the simplest of tasks. Bringing in the water, moving the baskets of grain, preparing my own meals, and dressing myself, just to name a few. For those who don't know me I had always been the man with the withered hand. They had never taken the time to find out my name or who I really was, just a man with his right hand withered.

"You can tell when people talk about you or ignore you. You feel their eyes on you, but they are afraid to make contact, to even say hello. My withered hand affected me in ways that at the time I didn't even realize. I viewed myself as somehow less than others because of the visible deformity.

"I never listened to those who said it was a result of my parents' sin, for they are righteous, God-fearing people. I, too, fear God and try to the best of my abilities to keep the commandments. Yet I always felt that I was singled out for some reason, some purpose. I knew intellectually that I was created and loved by God, for that is what the Law and the prophets teach, but I can admit now that internally I struggled with it. Then this Jesus bid me to stand in front of all those gathered.

"Silently, and with confidence, I did as He said. Jesus and I then exchanged a simple smile as I came forward. I could feel every eye on me as Jesus spoke to the crowd. Honestly, I forget exactly what He said, all I remember is an awkward silence that seemed to last a lifetime.

"I remember Jesus shaking His head in disappointment, and then, while looking at the Pharisees, He said to me, 'Stretch out your hand.'

"It was the most unbelievable feeling in the world," says the infamous man whom Jesus has healed. "It was as if the muscles and tendons and whatever else is inside my arm and hand released their grip, and then my hand, for the first time in my life, straightened out. I put my hands together in front of me and stared in amazement. Jesus touched my shoulder and then left the synagogue with His disciples close behind. I was in a state of shock; I didn't even get a chance to thank Him. My friends, family, and even total strangers approached and touched my restored hand.

"For the past week I have been called the man that Jesus touched; the man with the withered hand is a distant memory. Yet every time I embrace my wife, pick up my children to place them on my knee, put my hand to the plow, or reach for a piece of bread, I remember what Jesus did for me."

*****

One of the things I like most about this man, the man with the restored hand, is that he was in the synagogue; he was with the worshiping community. Despite his apparent deformity, he continued to worship and place himself in the presence of God, the Torah, and the faithful. It was not likely that sheer chance had brought him into the synagogue that day, but rather a pattern of faithfulness, which was noticed and used by Jesus to glorify God. This man had put himself in a position where he made himself available to God. He was also listening to Jesus, another detail that should not be lost.

Luke tells us that this man's right hand was withered, an important detail, because it was most likely the hand with which he would have worked. A damaged limb in first-century Middle Eastern society would have most likely reduced this man to a life of begging. However, he was not identified as begging in the streets or near the synagogue entrance but was in the synagogue. We can easily imagine others in the same situation calling God to judgment instead of worshiping Him. This man had a deep and abiding faith.

I admire how Jesus took the initiative in the synagogue. While Jesus was teaching, He was also keenly aware of the needs of the people before Him. Jesus wasn't preoccupied with how He appeared or the magnificence of the sermon. He noticed the man with the withered hand and called him up in front of the people. Luke doesn't even tell us what Jesus taught about that day or what portion of the Torah was read. What Luke does record is Jesus' actions, more so than His words.

The man with the withered hand answered Jesus' call, just as profoundly and faithfully as anyone in the gospel. He did as Jesus said. He was obedient and he risked being embarrassed and being the center of attention.

There were others who were conspicuously and noticeably silent that day in the synagogue—the scribes and Pharisees. However, their silence sprung from cowardice and a refusal to see the truth that was right in front of their eyes. They were so blinded by their legalistic point of view that they failed to recognize who was in their midst.

I would love to have been in the synagogue that day to see the contrast between the silent man with the withered hand and the silent Pharisees. I do, however, have to ask myself what I can learn from the example of this man, whose identity was wrapped up in his disability.

Where is Jesus calling us to stand up in faith and come forward? Where is He asking us to come up publicly and take a stand? There are many opportunities for this, but I believe that it does take a discerning spirit and perhaps some spiritual direction in order for us to do so.

I don't think that standing up for our faith means that we need to do something outrageous or tactless. It must begin with prayer and listening to the voice of God as it comes to us through the tradition of the Church and Scripture. When Jesus calls us, however, will we respond? Will we defend our faith when it is attacked? Will we stand up for the poor and those who may be marginalized by society? Will we come forward to speak for those who may have no voice in society? These are ways that we can make a difference both with and without words.

At this point in my life I have to ask myself how I have been doing in the above areas. Have I stood up for the poor and marginalized? Have I defended the faith when it was attacked or misrepresented? Without going into great detail, I can say that I need to work on some of those areas. How about you?

Could it be that God is calling you to something that you never thought possible? Have you placed yourself in a position where you are available to be used, to be a witness to God's grace and love? Is there a religious vocation that you are discerning? Is there a church with which you should be involved, or a Bible study or prayer group? Are there outreach organizations with which you can volunteer? Have your time and talents been offered to the church community? Are there magazines that encourage and defend the faith to which you should subscribe? The answers to these questions are between you and God, of course, but I do believe that God is searching for men and women, the old and the young, who are willing to be part of a community and stand up to come forward in faith.

There is a good chance that the work God calls you to do will be behind the scenes; that's where most of the work gets done anyway. Yet when God calls you, will you be ready, will you have the quiet confidence to stand for your faith? I believe you will, and so does God.

This man, identified by his deformity even after his healing, had his hand restored by the words of Christ. Jesus noticed and healed. Imagine the work you and I can do together. Is there a broken heart you can mend? Is there a lax faith you can help restore by your witness? Consider the countless ways that God can use you to bring restoration to the world.

If you hear Jesus calling you in the silence of your heart, do what He says. Reach out to God and others in faith regardless of your physical condition, because a miracle may be imminent!

TWENTY-THREE

The Silence of the Searchers

Luke 15:4-6, 8, 20

What man among you having a hundred sheep and losing one of them would not leave the ninety-nine in the desert and go after the lost one until he finds it? And when he does find it, he sets it on his shoulders with great joy and, upon his arrival home, he calls together his friends and neighbors and says to them, "Rejoice with me because I have found my lost sheep." ... Or what woman having ten coins and losing one would not light a lamp and sweep the house, searching carefully until she finds it?... So he got up and went back to his father. While he was still a long way off, his father caught sight of him, and was filled with compassion. He ran to his son, embraced him and kissed him.

In chapter fifteen of Luke's Gospel, Jesus tells three parables where the emphasis has been placed on the "lost": the lost sheep, the lost coin, and the lost son. It can be argued that each new parable highlights and increases the value of the "lost" and the importance of the "one gone astray"; one out of one hundred sheep, one of ten coins, and—the most significant—one of two sons. Animals, then money, and finally a son are used to heighten the value and importance of the lost.

Upon closer examination you could argue that the real emphasis is not on the "lostness" of the sheep, coin, or son, but rather on the silent, costly love shown by the one who seeks—namely, God.

The first parable Jesus addresses to the Pharisees and scribes is in response to their complaint that he eats with tax collectors and sinners. It is the parable of the seeking shepherd, in which a man, having one hundred sheep, loses one of them and seeks after it until he finds it. The story appears pretty simple, but let's take a closer look.

Jesus mentions that the man has one hundred sheep. It would have been highly unlikely that any one man would have owned one hundred sheep in Jesus' day. It was much more likely that the shepherd took care of the sheep belonging to many different people.

Imagine a man named John having ten sheep; Jacob, thirty-five; Isaac, twenty; and so on. It would be the hired shepherd's responsibility to watch and care for them all. When news went out that one was missing, it could be anyone's sheep that was missing. If it were John's sheep that was lost, then that would be 10 percent of his flock, which would be significant to John.

The good shepherd seeks the lost one, leaving the ninety-nine together in the comfort and security of each other's presence. They sense that if they are ever separated from the flock then the good shepherd will seek after them as well. The lost, solitary sheep will be petrified in fear, unable to move, and will continuously make a loud bleating sound that will alert and attract predators to his situation.

The good shepherd seeks the lost sheep. This is by no means a walk in the park. The desert is full of dangers and unforeseen hazards.

He will have to expose himself to the rugged terrain, where a twisted ankle could mean starvation or even heat stroke. Wild animals still roamed the land in Jesus' day; lions, wolves, and vultures were common. They were fierce predators of the meek and timid sheep and could bring harm to the shepherd as well.

This search is risky and dangerous. But this particular shepherd seeks out the lost sheep, listening for its cries and making haste lest predators arrive first.

The good shepherd, after finding the lost sheep, places it on his shoulders and begins his trek home. Can you imagine placing a seventy- or one-hundred-pound sheep on your shoulders and then carrying it a long distance in the hot Middle Eastern sun, through the desert and the fields? This is real labor, yet the good shepherd does exactly this, in silence and with great joy, and the people rejoice because the lost one is restored to the flock.

In the second parable Jesus uses the example of a woman to reveal what God's seeking love is like. This time the stakes are higher than a lost sheep; here we have money. Ten percent of this woman's dowry—which was commonly worn around the neck—has been lost.

In the town of Capernaum, where Jesus often made his home, the houses were made from the local black basalt rock. Archaeologists tell us that the homes had few if any windows, thus making the interior very dark to the naked eye. This detail is important because the woman in the parable searches *and* sweeps the house.

She would sweep in order to hear the coin rattle, and she would light her lamp because she couldn't see in the dark interior. You can almost picture her, bent over, with her lamp in one hand and a short broom in the other, looking, sweeping, listening. She, too, rejoices after the search is over and the coin is found.

The last and perhaps most famous of the three parables is that of the "Prodigal Son," or, to put it another way, the seeking father. Without a word, the father's loving action displays protective and costly love for his returning, though still lost, son. We are not told how long the son was away, but this only adds to the agony that the father had to endure as he waited and sought his son's return.

In the parable we hear the words of the younger son as he requests permission to leave and to take his share of the inheritance. This demand is unheard of in a Middle Eastern culture where the honor and respect for a father is held as one of the supreme virtues. Customary behavior dictates that the younger son would never speak this way to his father.

In fact, this son is acting as if his father is already dead. This father does not beat his insubordinate son, as would be expected, however. Amazingly, he gives him his share and lets him go.

We then read that the younger son collects all his belongings and sets off for a distant country. What is not recorded in the text, but would have been understood by the listeners of this parable, is that in this situation the townspeople would have been very aware of all that went on. They would have done great harm to the son if they ever got their hands on him for shaming the father and their village by his shameful behavior. This only highlights the public actions of the father a few scenes later.

The son, after ending up in a famine-stricken country with a job feeding pigs, comes to his senses but wants to *earn* his way back into his father's good graces by being a hired hand. He still doesn't get it. He views himself as a servant and not as a son.

This father catches sight of his son while the son is "still a long way off." The action of the father is astonishing in light of his Middle Eastern background. The father runs.

This simple action does not seem too absurd or astonishing to Western ears and eyes. But to Jesus' audience it certainly raised eyebrows, for rarely if ever do men in the Middle East run. Running is a sign that your affairs are out of order. There is a saying in the Middle East that says that you can tell a man by his walk. A man who walks at a slow, even gate has his dealings in order and is dignified.

Another problem for a man running was the awkwardness of his attire. For a man to run he would have to lift up his cloak, thus exposing his bare legs, which was dishonorable. Yet in this story the father, a wealthy landowner with servants, publicly runs out to his son, embraces him, and kisses him.

Before a word is spoken, his actions send a message to the townspeople who may plan to do harm to the son. The message is this: "I receive him back as a son, so hands off." The robe, ring, and sandals are only the outward signs of the father's acceptance and love; his sonship is restored by grace, and he has not earned it because it has come to him as a gift.

How long the father waited we can only imagine. What he thought about is another mystery. One thing is clear, nevertheless; that the father's seeking, running, and protection display that his love for his son is more important than any seemingly dishonorable behavior. He doesn't care what others think or to what honorable codes of conduct he may be acting in opposition; his son is returning.

Unlike the sheep or the coin in the first two parables, the son on his own volition decides to come home. Granted, his prospects were slim and his motivation, earning his way back, misguided. But he did come to his senses.

What was it that caused the father to run? Love, of course, but it wasn't intellectual, well thought-out words that convinced the father to run. It was just the sight of his son. Before a word is spoken by the son, the father is all over him, welcoming him back home.

Two things that come across in all of these parables are the costly love of the seeker as expressed in his or her sacrifice and the silence in which that person seeks. However, what is often unnoticed is the cost involved in the seeking. The joy on earth and in heaven due to the return of the lost certainly outweighs the cost of seeking, but there is a cost, there is the cross.

There is a temptation to think that somebody must come along and speak a fantastic sermon in order for the lost to be found. Have you ever wished that somebody else were there to talk to your "lost" friend? Certainly Fr. So-and-So would have the answers. Maybe if Sister were present she would know what to say.

At the same time, those who preach may sometimes take upon themselves too much pressure or credit for the return of the lost. Yet often the preaching is just one step in bringing a person "home." The labor beforehand of fasting, praying, and witnessing through living a holy life may go unrecognized by others, but not by God. These are vital for the conversion of anyone. It is a seeking heart that is inspired by the God who continues to speak in the quiet of the heart and who values the demanding and difficult nature of seeking.

What does that seeking look like today? I believe that it must begin with a prayerful heart and a missionary mind-set, because we should always be on the lookout for those to whom we can witness through our actions. It also takes fortitude, because it is no less difficult to witness through our actions than it is to carry a hundred-pound sheep through the rocky terrain of Israel! In fact, sometimes I wish it just involved physical labor to bring back the "lost."

I don't want to underestimate the power of words, because when we are asked about our faith, we had better have something meaningful to say. St. Peter himself reminds us, "Always be ready to give an explanation to anyone who asks you for a reason for your hope, but do it with gentleness and reverence, keeping your conscience clear, so that, when you are maligned, those who defame your good conduct in Christ may themselves be put to shame" (1 Pt 3:15-16).

I think of those who do all the behind-the-scenes work, the preparation that goes unnoticed unless it's not done. The countless hours put in by people who plan conferences and write bulletins; the youth ministers who reach out to the youth, those who plan Bible studies and visit the sick. The dedicated people who fill the food pantry, listen to the hopeless, befriend the lonely, and pray for the Church are all out there seeking the lost. Without a word, their work is the backbone of ministry.

Think of those who have brought you to where you are today. They usually don't brag or complain about their work. Some of them may have influenced you by their words, but most likely it was their example that was backed up by their words.

The shepherd first and foremost *noticed* that a sheep was missing. How do you feel when you are noticed, when somebody notices that you weren't present or that you look down? How did the shepherd know—there were so many of them, and didn't they all pretty much look the same?

This shepherd is different; he knows that they are not all the same, he knows their differences and tendencies, and he knows when even one is missing from the flock. Are there any sheep in your life? Somebody perhaps who has stopped showing up for Mass or a group meeting?

What happened to that person? What will it cost to seek him or her out? A phone call to let that person know that he or she is missed, a visit to that person's house, or even an invitation to your house for a meal?

In some cases you may be the only witness to Jesus that a person has. You certainly can't force a person to do something that he or she doesn't want to do, but you can definitely let that person know that you care, and offer an open invitation to him or her.

Those who have contact with youth know that young people are not all the same; each one is unique. Youth often get stereotyped by adults as being wild, "hormone crazy," and uncontrollable. Many adults do everything in their power to separate themselves from this group until they are more mature. But this is a grave error.

Young people bring with them a variety of differences and gifts that the Church needs. To treat them all the same does a great disservice to the Church community and to the youth themselves. We don't want them to get lost, especially when they have a tendency to wander from the community.

Most of us aren't familiar with the work of shepherds, but if we were, we would know that the shepherd can usually be seen in three locations with the sheep. The first is up ahead of them, in order to lead. The second location is toward the back of the flock, in order to encourage the stragglers; sometimes they need a kick in the rear.

The most common position, however, is right in their midst. This way the shepherd can get to know his flock. The same is true for people: We need to know when to lead, when to encourage, and when to just offer our presence.

The woman who was seeking the coin used both her eyes and her ears in seeking. What have you been seeing and hearing lately? Can you hear the "lostness" in some of your colleagues' and acquaintances' casual conversations?

Maybe it's not as obvious as the person who is habitually getting drunk or "wasted" every weekend, but if you are sensitive you may be able to sense when a person may be hurting or indirectly looking for assistance. Your eyes can glimpse the sadness in another's eyes. You may be able to perceive by a person's appearance or demeanor that something is wrong.

Our individual job is not to save everybody in the world, but if we are open to the Spirit we can be a force for good in helping and witnessing to others about our faith and hope. There is darkness inside of some people similar to the darkness inside of the woman's house. God calls us to be a light for them and a guide to bring them out of their darkness.

Finally, we see the actions of the father, an example of pure grace. Are there people in your life who have gravely offended you and have possibly wished you dead? How are you seeking them?

This is a challenging thought, indeed, and it makes me wonder about my own behavior toward those with whom I may not get along. It is a thought worth thinking about, in light of the father's action. He takes the initiative. He publicly runs out in the sight of everybody in order to reconcile himself with his son, a son who not only squandered property but also, more importantly, squandered a relationship. He broke the father's heart.

If we take a minute or two, I'm sure we may can think of a person who has really offended us, hurt us, and wounded us deeply. I'm sure there are a hundred reasons that we can come up with as to why we shouldn't forgive that person and be reconciled. There will be people who will nod their head in agreement at our justified anger.

We will think of countless reasons why not to be reconciled, but held up against the father's action, what choice is there? In some situations it may be humanly impossible for us to forgive, but then we need to call on the grace of God and the Holy Spirit to help us begin the process. It may not occur overnight, but it is a divine act to forgive and it takes humility and love to accept the forgiveness.

There is a growing ecumenical and interfaith movement within faith communities to heal old wounds that have divided Christians and people of other beliefs for centuries. This dialogue is called for by the Magisterium, the teaching authority of the Church, and is a movement of the Spirit.

There is a cost associated with reaching out to others, even today. People may not understand our actions, may question our motives, and may basically let broken relations and hurts remain. To follow Jesus, however, is to take risks, and to reach out to others is an essential element of discipleship.

I highly doubt that my emphasis on the *seeking* shepherd, the *seeking* woman, and the *seeking* father will have an impact on how the parables are introduced in the headings for these scriptural texts that appear in the lectionary. However, the next time you hear the parables of the lost sheep, the lost coin, and the lost son, remember the silent nature of the seekers and use your ears, eyes, and everything God has given you to seek the lost. In the end, this is the only thing that will really ever matter.

Let us look to Jesus in His example, and let our seeking be motivated by love. Then, with the good shepherd, with the woman with her coin, and with the father we will rejoice with the angels in heaven. Imagine the reception we'll receive!

TWENTY-FOUR

Thirty-Eight Years of Illness and the Glance of Christ

John 5:5-6

One man was there who had been ill for thirty-eight years. When Jesus saw him lying there and knew that he had been ill for a long time, he said to him, "Do you want to be well?"

Jesus asks a ridiculous question to an ill man, sick for thirty-eight years. Yes, I said it, ridiculous. "Do you want to be well?"

Of course the man wanted to be well. He wanted to be made whole, he wanted a normal life. Unfortunately, he thought that healing came from a pool rather than the touch of God.

But I'm getting ahead of myself. What comes before Jesus speaks is just as important as His words. That's what I'd like us to consider.

The Gospel writers take it for granted that the reader is somewhat familiar with the geography and layout of the land and the places that they write about. When comparing similar stories from the different Gospel writers, we find that they themselves are not always exact in telling us the placement of the story.

This is not the case, however, in St. John's recounting of the healing at the pool at Bethesda. We know where it was and have archeological evidence to back up the account. In fact, you can visit the ruins today. If you take a trip to Jerusalem you can see where the five colonnades were and you can even touch the water.

What is interesting is that this pool is right outside the Sheep Gate in Jerusalem, in the shadow of the northeast corner of the temple. There is a spring that runs under the pool that explains the extraordinary and sporadic stirring of the water that the people believed would heal them if they were the first ones in. St. John records that Jesus was going up to Jerusalem for a feast and passed through the gate. What would it have been like for the sick people who stayed and brought themselves there each day or were carried along with their hopes?

*****

The stirring and moans of the sick people awakened Benjamin from his sleep. He had not slept well; how could he with the constant sounds of wailing and sobbing all around him? These sounds were not unusual, but that didn't make it any easier for him to endure the night.

Benjamin was strong in faith, although his fault was to place his trust in almost anything or anyone who would pay him the slightest amount of attention. It was this faith that brought him to the pool in hopes of a cure.

"Maybe today, Benjamin," voiced an unusually upbeat Hagaba, who himself had been crippled. "Perhaps the water will stir and we will be cured."

"Wouldn't that be nice?" replied Benjamin. "Do you know, Hagaba, the first thing I'm going to do if I'm healed?"

"No, what is that?"

"I'm going to run and run until I can't run anymore."

"That would be nice. Maybe I'll join you and we'll race!"

They started laughing, which brought attention to them. Laughter was uncommon in this place of sickness and suffering. Hope is what they all held on to like a tree limb hanging from a cliff; if they let go of it they would fall into despair and then it would be only a matter of time before they wasted away.

"Watch it," shouted Benjamin as a blind man walked right into him, knocking over his drinking cup. No reply came from the blind man's lips.

"I shouldn't be surprised, Hagaba, this goes on every day. You know for yourself, getting walked into, walked on, bumped into. It bothers me occasionally, but do you know what really bothers me?"

"What really bothers you, my friend?"

"Let me tell you. I know a blind man can't see me and he doesn't walk into me on purpose, and some of the people around the pool have difficulties of their own. I can understand that. What gets under my skin is right over there, about two hundred yards away." He pointed to the stairs leading up to the temple.

Looking toward the temple, Hagaba replied, "What's over there that causes you such hardship? All I see are Pharisees, scribes, and Sadducees going up to the temple."

"Exactly," replied an excited Benjamin, "Exactly!"

Benjamin continued, "All day long I sit here suffering along with these other people, and not once have any of the 'religious leaders' come over and offered any assistance. Not even once!"

Hagaba reflected aloud, "I understand what you mean. They go to the temple to worship God as if God were not present in their midst through us. I know that sounds crazy, that God is present in us, but couldn't they at least talk to us, comfort us, or maybe help us into the pool? Would that be so difficult? Even Job had a few friends visit him in his suffering, and didn't the prophet Isaiah say something about comforting God's people?"

Looking around at the other sick people, Benjamin said, "I can deal with my illness, for I have been sick for thirty-eight years, but I can't stand to be treated as a nobody, as if I didn't even exist."

As Jesus was approaching the temple he looked to His right and stopped. In the distance Jesus saw a mass of sick people lying around the pool. He remembered when He was a child and had gone to Jerusalem with his mother and father. They had stopped to give alms to the poor in this area.

Jesus, without hesitation, made His way toward these people.

As Benjamin was about to speak, Jesus' gaze fell upon him and Jesus spoke to him, "Do you want to be well?"

The simple words startled the sick man momentarily; no one had ever been so simple and direct with him before, ever. Then he thought, *Do I want to be well? Why of course I want to be well. I've been sick for thirty-eight years! Do you think that I like sitting here with all of these sick people? What kind of question is that?*

The sick man, however, looked up at Jesus and replied respectfully, "Sir, I have no one to put me into the pool when the water is stirred up: while I am on my way, someone else gets down there before me."

Jesus said to him, "Rise, take up your mat, and walk."

Immediately he picked up his mat and walked.

To the surprise and wonderment of everybody, he walked. And then, looking to Hagaba, he started to run.

*****

This story is certainly miraculous. The details of the encounter, the length of time of the man's sickness, and the fact that it occurred on the Sabbath illuminate the miraculous touch of Christ. I would like to consider, however, the look of Jesus, for He noticed the sick man—He saw him.

The Gospel writer tells us that the man had been sick for thirty-eight years, an exceptional amount of time, considering that the average life expectancy was roughly forty-five years. Jesus saw him and stopped. How many others had walked on by? How many others went to offer sacrifice, to study the Law, and walked past all of these sick people? How many religious people walked right by in order to fulfill their "religious obligation" but failed to see the suffering in their midst?

Bible scholars tell us that most people in Jesus' day viewed suffering as a result of personal sin, so that might be an explanation for why people walked by. Their disposition could have been that these sick people deserved what they had received; therefore they were of no concern.

Jesus teaches us otherwise. Jesus stopped and spoke to this sick man. He took the initiative and made contact.

Before Jesus even said a word His actions must have broken with the normal behavioral code of a first-century rabbi. While Jesus was going to the temple to honor God, He did not fail to see God's presence in people, especially the sick, outcast, and marginalized. What a powerful message this sent to the disciples, that no one is outside the scope of God's love. God's love is extended to all, regardless of whether their suffering is caused by their own sin.

What a powerful message His actions also sent to those who were sick! "Here is someone," they concluded, "who cares and notices our sickness. While everybody else walks by, this man stops."

Jesus healed the man and ordered him to take up his mat and walk. And he did. What can this story teach us today? We might be thinking that if we had miraculous power then we, too, would stop to offer assistance. But until that should happen, what could we do?

The reality is that we can do great things and we can make a difference. It starts with noticing others and adopting the attitude of Jesus.

Jesus was going to a religious feast in Jerusalem, the Holy City, the center for Jewish worship, yet before He entered the temple He took time to help a sick man. What was Jesus' priority? It's clear that the sick man came first.

There was no contradiction of priorities for Jesus. It was not a choice between God and the sick man, but apparently a choice to serve God *through* the sick man. Afterward, Jesus went on into Jerusalem to fulfill His religious duty, but not before He alleviated the suffering of a sick man.

I like the fact that Jesus wasn't pressed for time. So often I find myself running around here and there trying to keep up with my busy schedule and load of responsibilities, yet I read here that Jesus stopped. His actions conveyed clearly that He thought it was important to take time for the sick.

I wonder what my lifestyle and priorities communicate to those around me? What do my actions and use of time silently communicate to others? It's a scary thought if I really think about it, yet it brings to light the priorities people have in life, as expressed through their simple, daily actions.

I know Jesus walks with me on my journey, but I wonder: If Jesus were physically to walk with me through my day, where would He place His priorities? I'm starting to wonder if the things I believe are so important are the things that He thinks are so important. Come to think about it, I know the answer, and that should continue my on-going conversion.

The fact of the matter is that Jesus does walk with me through my day, and I have to be attentive to the Spirit's leading and prompting so as not to miss those people and opportunities that come my way.

What would Jesus say about your schedule? Are you spending an inordinate amount of time on things that are not very important? How about your religious obligations? Do you ignore people and push them out of your way in order to make it to church ten minutes early to pray? How do you discern God's will, even in the minutiae and finer points of your schedule?

With this in mind we can turn to the Church and the Scriptures for guidance and direction and we can also turn to those whom God has placed around us. God often speaks through others in the Scriptures and in our own lives. The gift of counsel can protect us from being guided by our own self-interest or from impulses that may serve our urges and selfish nature rather than the will of God.

Ask the Holy Spirit to move in your heart and convict you of any misplaced priorities. Ask the Holy Spirit for the eyes of Christ, that you may notice those around you who are suffering. Seek, too, the counsel of those you respect, for God can speak to you through them.

The Scriptures do not tell us the exact nature of this man's illness or even whether it was a physical problem. Some of the people you and I encounter each day will be similar to this man. We may not even be aware that there is a storm going on inside them, yet the power of our actions, noticing them and caring for them with or without words, and even just remembering their names, can be a very powerful witness and can mean more than a physical healing. After all, aren't there times when you and I long for somebody to notice us and provide for us a sense of community?

Of all the verses I've read in the Bible, I think this particular story contains the saddest words spoken in Scripture. These are pretty bold words, I know, but I do stand by that statement. These words are placed on the lips of the sick man and went totally unnoticed by me the first twenty or so times that I read the story.

These sad words are found in verse seven: "Sir, I have no one to put me into the pool when the water is stirred up." Can you believe that? In the shadow of the temple, in the Holy City of Jerusalem, here is a man who can utter the words, "Sir, I have no one ..."

No one to help me, no one who notices me, no one who cares. Are there people we come across in our daily walk who could speak those words? Hopefully not, if God has placed us in their presence. No one should ever be able to say those words if a Christian is present— no one.

I wonder what the real miracle was in this story—the physical healing of the man or the fact that Jesus saw him and stopped? I believe that they're both miraculous. I also believe that the silent actions of Jesus that Sabbath day can impact my life and give me pause to think more than can the physical healing itself.

Empowered from our encounter with Christ, we can bring His real presence to others through our actions. This gives me hope and assurance, because it tells me that Christ still continues to notice my burdens and me—even when others may be unaware through no fault of their own.

Jesus may have been a few minutes late for the feast, and the festivities may have begun without Him, but ask the sick man if he was happy that Jesus stopped that day. I'm sure that there are people in your life who can say the same thing: that their lives are better because you stopped and noticed them.

TWENTY-FIVE

Two Small Copper Coins

Mark 12:42

A poor widow also came and put in two small coins worth a few cents.

She wasn't noticed by the scribes and Pharisees, or by anyone else, for that matter. She was one of those individuals that people don't really observe or take note of. Although we might see her on the street or in the market, there was nothing extraordinary about her to make us take notice.

Nobody much cared where she was going or coming from. A nameless widow, seemingly preoccupied with her task at hand, going to the temple to place her two small coins in the treasury. This day, however, would be different, not so much for her as for the disciples, and for believers down through the centuries.

It was her regular routine, going to the temple, fulfilling her religious obligation. Long ago her husband had died, leaving her a widow. Nobody really remembered, or, for that matter, cared, what had happened to her children, or if she even had any. She continued to exist despite her meager living conditions and she joined the other widows and poor people along side of the road, selling anything from fruit and vegetables to articles of clothing that she stitched together with her aging hands.

Throughout her life she had relied on God's providence. Her age and financial status would not hinder her firm belief and sense of religious duty.

With her old clothes and worn sandals, she headed out the door, shuffling her feet and clutching two small coins tightly in her hand. She walked anonymously into the busy street leading up to the temple treasury, as she had done all her life. Crowds of people, all in a hurry, passed her by. She didn't notice them unless they carelessly bumped into her.

In the temple area, Jesus was surrounded by His disciples. A small number of scribes, elders, and Sadducees were absorbed in discussing the topics of the day. It was one debate after another as Jesus taught and fielded questions from the religious leaders.

As Jesus was walking in the temple area, the chief priests, the scribes, and the elders approached Him and said, "By what authority are you doing these things? Or who gave you this authority to do them?"

Jesus said to them, "I shall ask you one question. Answer me, and I will tell you by what authority I do these things. Was John's baptism of heavenly or of human origin? Answer me" (see Mk 11:27-30).

The small band of adversaries discussed the question among themselves and decided that it was better to remain silent for fear of the crowds. So they said to Jesus in reply, "We do not know."

Then Jesus said to them, "Neither shall I tell you by what authority I do these things" (Mk 11:33).

Jesus then told the parable of the tenants to them, and as angry as they were with Him, these "antagonists" left, for fear of the crowds.

Seeking to trap Jesus in His own speech, some Pharisees and Herodians approached and tested Jesus on the question of taxes. Jesus amazed them with His teaching, but then some Sadducees arrived and questioned Him about the resurrection and the greatest commandment.

Then, in the course of His teaching, Jesus warned the disciples to beware of the hypocrisy of the scribes.

It was at this point that Jesus sat down, perhaps fatigued from the constant defense of His teaching and the verbal battles with the scribes.

The Master Teacher was about to teach one of His greatest lessons, and it was going to come from an unusual source: an unnamed, poor widow!

Jesus, sitting opposite the treasury, observed how the people were putting money into the treasury. We are told that the rich people were putting in large sums. We can only imagine the show they made of it and the performance they put on for the others to see. From a distance it was clear to those in the vast temple treasury area who was putting what into the coffers.

Jesus watched. What was He looking for? What were the people putting in large sums looking for—praise from their peers, admiration from the poor, commendation from God? His disciples must have noticed the disgust on His face as Jesus shook His head from side to side.

At the clanging of two small copper coins, Jesus had witnessed what He was looking for. He called over His disciples. A teaching moment was not lost.

Jesus said to His disciples, "Amen, I say to you, this poor widow put in more than all the other contributors to the treasury. For they have all contributed from their surplus wealth, but she, from her poverty, has contributed all she had, her whole livelihood."

*****

In first-century Middle Eastern society you couldn't get much lower on the social ladder than a poor widow. Yet she didn't escape the eyes of Jesus. No act of sacrifice or love escapes His eyes. Her silent contribution was remembered by the Christian community and recorded in the Gospels, for she placed not only her money in the treasury but also her trust in God.

In silence Jesus watched. In silence the poor widow placed her coins in the treasury. Where does this event leave you and me? Challenged, I hope, for as Jesus' disciples we are called to follow this widow's example as well as His and to place our trust in God.

Yet how do we do this? What might following her example look like for us today?

I believe that we must start by prayer—a humble and sincere heart asking God what areas of our lives we need to surrender, and in which areas we need to give all.

Certainly being generous with our money can be a blessing for the Church and can enable some godly work to continue. The missions, soup kitchens, and food pantries, as well as the parish's operating budget, need the financial generosity of the parishioners.

Nevertheless, the primary question is this: To what is God calling you? To what is He calling you to give all? And how are you responding? Are you looking for praise from others, or, like the widow, are you giving humbly and generously?

Most people give to their church financially, but are there other areas in which God is calling you to give generously? It can be easier to place your money or envelope in the collection basket without really being honest with God and asking Him to what He wants you to give your all.

For myself, it is often how I spend my time that is a challenge. I think of this teaching moment of Jesus and ask myself how I give of my time—to my family, work and relationships, relaxation and prayer?

When Jesus looked at this widow, He saw more than her outward appearance. He saw the widow's heart through her generosity. How do I view people?

I need to ask Jesus to give me His eyes so that I can begin to look at others the way He does. Perhaps I need to give up all of my attitudes toward others and my pride that prevents others from seeing God in me.

Maybe it's the way I look at people who might be considered "outcasts" or marginalized by society. Am I lavish with my praise of others, and do I boast about the goodness of others, whether they are friends, coworkers, or employees? Do I only extol myself in order to make up for my low self-esteem?

It's truly amazing what can begin to happen in others when we notice them and praise them publicly. Whatever approach to giving we may take, it should start with prayer and silence. From there God will let us know. Then we must follow His leading.

Another thing that fascinates me about this story is that Jesus did not stop the widow in the story to praise her personally. She was not called over and given a pat on the back. Why didn't Jesus affirm her personally, face-to-face?

The answer, I think, is that she didn't need it. She knew that she was doing the right thing, and that was enough. God had taken care of her up to this point, and He would continue to provide for her needs in the future. I'd like to think that there was some communication such as a wink or a smile on Jesus' behalf, but that probably reflects my own need to be affirmed rather than the widow's.

Quietly, Jesus watched and taught His disciples that this is the type of faith God is asking for—not the self-righteous actions of the scribes and the lengthy prayers of the Pharisees, but the humble sacrifice of the widow.

Whatever the world may be doing, we can be assured that God is watching and that He is pleased with our desire to give everything over to Him. The response to His call may look different for each of us, but let our silent actions be a sermon and an example for others.

TWENTY-SIX

A Woman With an Alabaster Jar

Luke 7:37-38

Now there was a sinful woman in the city who learned that he was at table in the house of the Pharisee. Bringing an alabaster flask of ointment, she stood behind him at his feet weeping and began to bathe his feet with her tears. Then she wiped them with her hair, kissed them, and anointed them with the ointment.

Simon, a Pharisee, invited Jesus to come and eat with him. Jesus accepted his offer, and this ordinary meal would be forever transformed, not by what was served by Simon but by the words of Jesus and the actions of a woman who is only described as sinful. What transpired at this supper would be remembered and retold by the Christian community for generations to come. The silent, unnamed woman, through her lavish, loving actions, would be forever remembered for her faith and the love that she poured out to Jesus, and not for her sinfulness.

* * * * *

The synagogue service had ended and the Pharisees, along with some scribes, remained afterward, as was their custom, to discuss and argue the finer points of the Law. Fingers were pointed, hands were thrown up in the air, voices were raised, and the Torah was quoted, along with the interpretations of famous rabbis; they couldn't have been more content.

News that Jesus had been teaching and preaching locally had reached the religious leadership in the community. The "common" people, the people of the land, were attracted to Jesus' message and they were talking about Him quite openly. The Pharisees and teachers of the Law were beginning to become disturbed by Jesus' popularity, as well as the people's reaction to Him.

As the Pharisees and teachers of the Law finally broke up their impromptu discussion and began to go their separate ways, Simon looked over to Jehoram and nodded for him to come over. "All is ready," he uttered quietly, for fear of being too loud. "The invitation has been made and Jesus has accepted. Perhaps He is a prophet from God. If not, however, we will show this Galilean 'Teacher' the way things are done."

Jehoram agreed with a smile and added, "I'll make sure that He receives no special treatment and that He reclines at the *end* of the table. I'm tired of these so-called teachers claiming to speak for God when they have not even approached us, the officially authorized teachers who have been trained in the Scriptures!"

Simon agreed with a sneer and stroked his beard. "This Jesus will soon understand whom He is dealing with and the way things are carried out." An unexpected smile appeared on Simon's face as he continued, "Have no fear, Jehoram, He *will* get the message."

The day for the meal soon arrived. The invited guests entered and received the expected display of hospitality, the greeting with a kiss, the offer of water for the feet, and the invitation to recline around the table near the host. These simple acts of hospitality were provided with the usual care to all—with the exception of Jesus.

To their surprise, Jesus didn't say a word. He took a seat at the far end of the table and began to talk to those next to Him.

Simon, wondering why Jesus didn't protest this mistreatment, looked over at Jehoram, who himself had not taken his eyes off Jesus. His gaze said, *Just wait, just give it time, He'll break.* Simon dipped his bread into the stew and leaned back to eat. The other Pharisees and scribes were quite aware of the awkward mistreatment of this Galilean visitor, as were the other people who had taken seats against the back wall of the dining area, as was the custom.

"Simon," whispered Jehoram, "could this 'teacher' be oblivious to the way we're treating Him? He's an even bigger fool than I had imagined."

Jehoram leaned back and relaxed, and with a slight smile he whispered, "We have nothing to worry about from this 'teacher.'"

As the words were leaving his lips, the door opened and a woman entered the room. At once every eye was on her. Drinking cups hit the tabletop as jaws dropped. The woman was scantily dressed, and subsequently the men didn't know whether to stare at her or to look away politely. Most of them had seen her before, and to some of those gathered she was more than an acquaintance.

She wiped the tears from her eyes as she wept and made her way over to Jesus. The smell of her expensive perfume permeated the air as she made her way straight to His feet. She dropped down to her knees and fumbled for the flask that hung around her neck.

Out of the ornamented and delicately fashioned alabaster flask poured a sweet-scented ointment with which she bathed His feet. The weeping continued as the conversations and eating came to a dead stop. An uncomfortable silence hung in the air; the stunned guests at the dinner party were flabbergasted.

Is this the kind of person who keeps company with Jesus? they thought but were too polite to say. *Oh, the scandal!* thought others, as their eye contact with each other brought snickers and sneers of disbelief.

If this man were a prophet, he would know who and what sort of woman this is who is touching him, that she is a sinner, thought Simon (see Lk 7:39), utterly amazed that Jesus would allow a sinner to touch Him, and a woman, no less!

Jesus said to him in reply, "Simon, I have something to say to you."

"Tell me, Teacher," he said.

"Two people were in debt to a certain creditor; one owed five hundred days' wages and the other owed fifty. Since they were unable to repay the debt, he forgave it for both. Which of them will love him more?"

Simon said in reply, "The one, I suppose, whose larger debt was forgiven."

He said to him, "You have judged rightly" (Lk 7:40-43).

Simon looked over at Jehoram, wondering where this conversation was going. Jehoram shrugged his shoulders and nervously turned his attention to Jesus, who was still reclining, calm and relaxed. Then Jesus did something that no one who witnessed it would ever, ever forget. Jesus publicly shamed Simon right in front of his guests and right in his own home. It was without a doubt unbelievable!

He turned to the woman and said to Simon, "Do you see this woman? When I entered your house, you did not give me water for my feet, but she has bathed them with her tears and wiped them with her hair. You did not give me a kiss, but she has not ceased kissing my feet since the time I entered. You did not anoint my head with oil, but she anointed my feet with ointment. So I tell you, her many sins have been forgiven; hence she has shown great love. But the one who little is forgiven, loves little."

He said to her, "Your sins are forgiven."

The others at the table said to themselves, *Who is this who even forgives sins?* But He said to the woman, "Your faith has saved you, go in peace" (Lk 7:44-50).

The room remained silent as Jesus touched her cheek with His hand and raised her up to her feet. Jesus took another sip of wine, nodded to Simon, who was in a state of shock, and left. Never before had Simon, a respected Pharisee, been spoken to in this way. It was as if somebody had slapped him in the face.

Silent in his reply to Jesus, he sat motionless. His shame was turning to anger. His guests excused themselves politely, along with the onlookers, amid a buzz of bewilderment.

*****

The meal ended for Simon and the unnamed silent woman, but I doubt that their lives were ever the same. I wonder: Was Simon, still burning from that public shaming, in Jerusalem calling for Jesus' death on that fateful Passover? Or did he think about the parable Jesus had told and change his ways— showing thankfulness to God for taking away the debt of sin in Jesus?

Simon had wanted to use this meal, not as a social gathering to listen to Jesus, but to put Him in His place. Throughout the Mediterranean region in Jesus' day, people would have eaten at a *triclinium*, a three-sided table where they reclined by resting their weight on their left sides and eating with their right hands. Their feet would have been pointing away from them, toward the outer walls of the room. This reclining posture symbolized their freedom, for slaves had to stand while eating.

Seating at the *triclinium* carried a certain social message, for it symbolized your status to those who ate with you at the table. It also sent a message to those who observed the meal in order to hear the religious teachers' views and applications of the Law. Those gathered could listen to the latest teaching and hear the scholars defend their interpretations of the Torah.

The host would sit in the second seat on the left of this horseshoe-shaped table, with the man on his right hand taking care of the details of the meal. Those gathered would then sit in order of importance, going from the greatest to least around the table. Jesus warned His disciples against giving special status to people and told them explicitly not to take the places of honor, but to go instead to the lowest place.

Hospitality, such as a kiss of peace or an offer of water for the feet, would be given to the guests. Today similar hospitality would include an offer to take a person's coat, a handshake, an embrace, or an offer of a cold beverage.

Jesus entered Simon's house and was not given even the basics of simple hospitality. This would be a glaring insult for anyone familiar with Middle Eastern hospitality. Simon was sending a message to Jesus without a word. Jesus did not mention the insult, and He did not storm out, as would be expected. Instead, He sat and listened.

It isn't complicated with this mental picture in mind to imagine the woman entering the room, going to Jesus' outstretched feet, and letting down her hair to dry the tears she has cried there. She showed Jesus the hospitality that was omitted by Simon. The Gospel writer tells us what Simon was thinking, but what do the woman's actions reveal about her thoughts? What drove her to this great show of unbridled and lavish affection?

Without a word she revealed her great love, as expressed in her actions. She poured out, unashamedly, publicly, in lavish fashion, all to Jesus. Her kisses, her tears, and her love were poured out at His feet. Five times Jesus' feet are mentioned in this story, and the woman's benevolent actions are heightened by this fact.

This woman was not concerned with what others were thinking. Certainly she was aware of what Simon and his guests were thinking, yet this did not stop her; she was not ashamed to express her love to Jesus publicly. That's what love does; it can't, by its very nature, hold back.

Tradition and evidence within the text have classified this nameless and wordless woman as a prostitute. If this is true, that she was a prostitute, we can assume she was a very successful one: Her alabaster jar of ointment would have been an expensive item in the Middle East at that time.

Prostitutes would use this fragrance to perfume their clients and themselves to cover the offensive smell that the heat and sweat would naturally bring. However, in a costly act of love, this woman publicly poured it and her heart out to Jesus. She would no longer need the ointment.

What a conversion, what faith this woman displayed! No wonder Jesus responded in such a forceful way to Simon after He told him a parable about two debtors. Much as the prophet Nathan had once confronted King David about his adultery and murder (see 2 Sm 12:1-15), Jesus brought Simon face-to-face with his sin.

What Jesus did at this meal in response to the sinful woman would have gotten Him in big trouble. Jesus, a young rabbi from the less respected northern area of Galilee, entered Simon's house and, in the presence of everybody, reprimanded Simon for not providing Him with the minimal amount of hospitality. What Jesus did by publicly shaming Simon was to make Simon look like a fool.

In Middle Eastern culture men do not take kindly to that. Honor and shame are two driving forces that still influence everything there from family life to politics.

Imagine yourself, if you will, as a character in the Mafia movie *The*

Godfather. Picture yourself sitting at a table with the Godfather and all his men. Now imagine a young guest saying to the Godfather, "This is the worst meal I've ever tasted, and your daughter is ugly!"

What would you be thinking? Most likely it would be something like, "This guy is crazy; he'll be sleeping with the fish before nightfall!" I guarantee you that you would never forget that night! Nor would the guests in the room with Simon and Jesus ever have forgotten the tension they experienced that night.

What can we learn from this woman who silently poured out her ointment, the tool of her trade, to Jesus? What do we need to "pour out" to Jesus? What do we need to empty ourselves of and lay at His feet?

Another question to consider is what may hold us back from giving our all to Jesus. Is there a temptation to hold something back? Do we feel the need to hold on to some sin?

This is an ongoing process for most of us, I'm sure. Little by little we may give Jesus more of our time or attention.

Perhaps there is an action or attitude that we need to pour out completely at Jesus' feet. Maybe a past sin or failure is holding us back from moving forward in our relationship with God. Maybe we are stingy or guarded and not extravagant with our affection toward Jesus and others.

Instead, we need to be like this woman, who was not afraid to let others know how she felt about Jesus. Her faith was not a private affair. Love cares little for what others think.

God may reveal to you what it is that you need to pour out so that you may be free from your old ways and alive for Him. You may know or sense in your heart what you need to do. Others can also be valuable in the process of letting go and pouring out. A spiritual advisor or the counsel of a friend or community can be the vehicle God uses to reveal to you an area of your life that is out of order.

You may not even be aware of an area of your life that prevents you from progressing in the spiritual life. Others may be able to enlighten you to this. Be open to the Spirit and to those around you.

Whatever your situation, ask the Holy Spirit to reveal what you may need to "pour out." As surely as the woman was assured of Jesus' love and forgiveness, so will He assure you of His love for you, that you, too, may be free and "go in peace."